$34.50
$31.05 w/mailer

ODYL

THE URBAN LANDSCAPE:
HISTORICAL DEVELOPMENT AND
MANAGEMENT

THE URBAN LANDSCAPE: HISTORICAL DEVELOPMENT AND MANAGEMENT

PAPERS BY M. R. G. CONZEN

INSTITUTE OF BRITISH GEOGRAPHERS
SPECIAL PUBLICATION, NO. 13

Edited by

J. W. R. WHITEHAND

Department of Geography,
University of Birmingham

1981

ACADEMIC PRESS
A Subsidiary of Harcourt Brace Jovanovich, Publishers
London   New York   Toronto   Sydney   San Francisco

ACADEMIC PRESS INC. (LONDON) LTD.
24/28 Oval Road,
London NW1

United States Edition published by
ACADEMIC PRESS INC.
111 Fifth Avenue
New York, New York 10003

British Library Cataloguing in Publication Data
The Urban landscape: historical development and
    management. – (Special publication/Institute of British
    Geographers, ISSN 0073–9006; 13)
    1.   City planning
    I.   Whitehand, J. W. R.
    711 .4   HT166

ISBN 0–12–747020–4

LCCCN 81–68018

Phototypeset by Rowland Phototypesetting Ltd,
Bury St Edmunds, Suffolk
and printed in Great Britain by
St Edmundsbury Press, Bury St Edmunds, Suffolk

PREFACE

During the last decade there has been increasing concern in western countries for the visual aspects of the environment, particularly from the point of view of its amenity value. This follows a period when the landscape generally, and perhaps the urban landscape in particular, has undergone great pressures for change. But anything approaching a coherent body of knowledge of urban landscape evolution that might form a basis or context for the policy of landscape management that this situation calls for is lacking and there is little prospect of piecing together a coherent picture from the diverse literature that has a bearing on the subject. This volume certainly does not attempt to do this but instead is concerned with one major line of evolution of research on the urban landscape that has borne major fruits yet is still only well known to a limited number of scholars. This line has its beginning in central Europe at the end of the nineteenth century and its principal recent development in Britain during approximately the last quarter of a century. The touchstone of this work is its morphogenetic character and its key exponent is M. R. G. Conzen. By far the best known of his publications is *Alnwick, Northumberland: a study in town-plan analysis*. It is regarded as a classic by most scholars working in the field of urban morphology, being arguably the first attempt in the English-language literature to place research in urban morphology on a systematic footing and successfully bridging the German–English language divide.

In spite of the exodus of scholars and scientists from German-speaking Europe in the 1930s, M. R. G. Conzen was the only German-trained geographer of the inter-war period to take up a university appointment in Britain on a permanent basis. A student in Berlin under Albrecht Penck and Norbert Krebs, he is the only direct link between British geography and the exceptionally fruitful period of German geography between the two world wars. His work has remained as unconforming in a British geography swamped by trans-Atlantic influences in the 1960s and 1970s as it was in one characterized by isolation, both international and inter-disciplinary, in the two preceding decades. From an international perspective it represents a significant link in the web of scholarly communication and influence and a rare entrée into a comparatively little known tradition. For geographers with interests in the physical character of urban areas it provides a source of ideas that has as yet been far from fully tapped and among historians and planners its potentialities remain largely unrealized.

The purpose of this volume is to bring to the wider attention of geographers, historians and town planners four of Conzen's papers published since 1960—when the Alnwick study appeared—that have hitherto been relatively inaccessible owing to the limited availability in Britain and America of the publications in which they originally appeared. These papers provide the core of the volume. They are preceded by an account of the antecedents and major characteristics of work in this tradition (Chapter 1) and followed by a discussion of attempts that have been made—mainly during the 1970s—to apply and develop Conzen's ideas and to examine their relationship to ideas stemming from different traditions (Chapter 6).

The four papers were originally published between 1962 and 1978 and bridge the period between the largely descriptive works that characterized urban morphology in the English-speaking world in the 1950s and the advent of the more interpretative and analytical approaches that were becoming more common during the 1970s, partly as a consequence of the spread of Conzen's ideas but also as a result of the permeation into the field of methods from the social sciences. The papers themselves are in virtually all respects as pertinent today as when they were written and no attempt has been made to up-date them. The one paper that appears in translation follows the original German version, with minor revisions by the author, and the other three papers are reproduced essentially in their original form, except that a small number of minor changes of wording have been made where these appeared to improve readability.

The first paper (Chapter 2), originally published in the Swedish serial *Lund Studies in Geography Series B*, applies the method previously developed in the English market town of Alnwick to the highly complex case of an English city centre. It was first presented at the International Geographical Union symposium on urban geography in Lund in 1960 at which it was followed by a discussion of the state of urban morphology to which W. L. Garrison and Conzen were contributors and which has been looked back on as in some way symbolizing a major phase of reassessment in urban morphology. The second paper (Chapter 3), first published in a *Festschrift* for G. H. J. Daysh, and the third (Chapter 4), originally published in *Giessener Geographische Schriften*, reflect Conzen's professional interest in town planning—he worked for a planning consultancy in the 1930s before becoming a professional geographer—and his concern that the concepts and methods of townscape analysis should play an integral part in town planning. The last and most recent paper (Chapter 5) was a contribution to a volume sponsored by the *Institut für Vergleichende Städtegeschichte* in Münster on problems of urbanism in the industrial era and draws together a number of important ideas in urban morphology, many of which are exemplified in the earlier papers.

The preparation of this volume has been greatly assisted by the efforts of a number of colleagues and friends. In particular I should like to record my thanks to Professor Michael P. Conzen of the Department of Geography, University of Chicago and Professor Kathleen Neils Conzen of the Department of History at the same institution for undertaking the initial translation from the German of the paper that comprises Chapter 5. The former was also responsible for the greater part of the cartography for Figs 2, 3, 17, 18 and 21 in that chapter and was a source of advice throughout the preparation of the volume. Members of the Urban

Morphology Research Group in the Department of Geography, University of Birmingham, in particular Messrs T. R. Slater, P. J. Aspinall, I. A. Thompson and R. J. Pain, provided a sounding-board for drafts of Chapters 1 and 6, and Mrs J. Dowling and Messrs R. C. Swift, G. Dowling and T. G. Grogan of the same department made major contributions to the restoration and, in many cases, complete redrafting of the artwork for Chapters 2 and 5. Finally, I owe an incalculable debt to Professor M. R. G. Conzen, not just for providing detailed and indispensable background information for Chapter 1, but more generally for affording me access through his scholarly discourses to intellectual avenues largely unexplored by English-speaking geographers.

August 1981   *J. W. R. Whitehand*
                                                        University of Birmingham

CONTENTS

ONE

Background to the urban morphogenetic tradition

J. W. R. WHITEHAND

The main line of post-war geographical research on the urban landscape—the Conzenian tradition—has its antecedence in the German-speaking countries. There a rich tradition of urban morphological research goes back to the turn of the century and it is there that we must look for the origins of the morphogenetic approach—the tracing of the evolution of forms in terms of their underlying formative processes—with which the name of M. R. G. Conzen has become so closely identified[1]* and which is the focus of attention in this volume.

Except in Conzen's own work, this German-language literature has for the most part received only perfunctory mention in the literature of other languages. Indeed, if it had not been for the work of Dickinson who, particularly in the 1940s, published several papers in English and American journals and a major book based heavily on German publications,[2] the work of geographers in central Europe would have been known to few scholars in Britain and America.

In the English-speaking and French-speaking countries, although the landscape generally has been the subject of a good deal of attention, if not as much as in the German-speaking lands, research on the *urban* landscape has been slow to develop. Indeed, for the period before the Second World War it is difficult to compile a bibliography of more than a score of geographical works emanating from America, Britain and France together that demonstrate a major concern with the urban landscape, the studies of Blanchard in France,[3] Fleure in Britain,[4] and Leighly in America[5] being among the few key ones to appear.

Conzen's ideas, which began to appear in British publications some years after his emigration from Germany to Britain in 1933, were slow to be assimilated by the few English-speaking geographers who were researching into urban morphology in the early post-war years. Even more recently, when his ideas have been vigorously taken up, the central European intellectual tradition from which they sprang has remained poorly understood. It is therefore to a consideration of this tradition that we must first turn.

---

* Superscript numbers refer to numbered notes at the end of each chapter.

Central European origins

Geographical research on the urban landscape in the German-speaking countries may be traced back at least to the early work of Schlüter, notably two papers published in 1899 when he was 26 years of age, one on the ground plan of towns[6] and the other his views on wider aspects of settlement geography,[7] and a monograph on the settlements of north-eastern Thuringia, published in 1903.[8] Also relevant are two later methodological publications, a discourse on the aims of human geography[9] and an essay on the place of human geography in geographical science.[10]

The second and fourth of these publications are particularly important because of their programmatic character and subsequent influence on the development of human geography in general and settlement geography in particular.[11] They were written at a time when human geography, under the impact of Ratzel's *Anthropogeographie*[12] with its potentially polyhistoric perspective, seemed likely to become a universal "science of relations" (*Beziehungswissenschaft*), boundless in its scope and extremely diverse in its objects. In Schlüter's view this was not only philosophically unsound but threatened the unity of geography as a properly determined subject within the developing system of sciences. Worse, it rendered human geography impossible as a manageable and purposeful major subdivision by arbitrarily restricting it to the investigation of man's dependence on nature.[13] To establish such a subdivision as human geography it was necessary to assign to it a distinct object of research not claimed by any other discipline. Von Richthofen had defined the central object of investigation in geography as the "earth's surface and the objects and phenomena causally connected with it",[14] and within physical geography this was already leading to the vigorous development of geomorphology. In analogy to this Schlüter now postulated a morphology of the "cultural landscape" (*Kulturlandschaft*) as the object of research in "cultural geography" (*Kulturgeographie*), for him the most important part of human geography.[15] He called for the detailed description of the visible and tangible man-made forms on the ground and their genetic and functional explanation in terms of the aims and actions of man in the course of history and in the context of nature.[16] From the beginning then he was not content with merely descriptive morphography but envisaged an explanatory morphology, being fully aware of the interdependence in geography of the three aspects of form, function and development (history).

Schlüter drew attention to settlements, land utilization and lines of communication as the three systematic kinds of objects comprising the cultural landscape and giving rise to three subdivisions of human geography, namely settlement geography, economic geography and transport geography.[17] In settlement geography the existence of rural and urban settlements provided the basis for a further subdivision. Within urban geography Schlüter regarded the physical forms and appearance of the town, the "urban landscape" (*Stadtlandschaft*), as the main object of research, viewing it as a distinct category of cultural landscape and as such a regional unit in its own right.[18] Thus a marked morphological emphasis was imparted to human geography in general and urban geography in particular that was to become increasingly evident over the first three decades of this century.

While Schlüter was undoubtedly a key figure influencing this trend, an important and in some ways distinctive, though eminently morphological, contribution came during the second decade of the century from Hassinger.[19] Concerned originally with the problems of preservation in the Old Town of Vienna and thus to a large extent with the distribution of architectural monuments, he mapped the historic architectural styles there, eventually extending this to include the whole of the city in his "art-historical" atlas of Vienna. Interesting and valuable for their purpose as these magnificent efforts were in showing the wealth of architectural monuments of a famous city and the danger to which they were exposed under modern metropolitan conditions, strictly speaking this mapping was not geographical but architectural or "art-historical" (*kunsthistorisch*), as indeed the titles of all the publications up to the middle of the First World War indicated. It was only after that war that this type of work came to be called "art geography" (*Kunstgeographie*) in the publications of Hassinger's pupil Schaefer.[20] Predictably, perhaps inevitably in view of the widespread interest in morphological issues elsewhere in central Europe during the 1920s, the new term became the subject of methodological controversy. It was one thing to map house types in a way that captured the basic connotations of function and period of origin—whatever this implied in terms of architectural style—and quite another to map a single aspect like artistic style in isolation. It is interesting that Hassinger himself broadened the geographical perspective by giving greater attention to land and building utilization and residential densities in his study of Basel.[21]

However, in the long term probably the most influential works of the early inter-war years sprang from the foundations that had already been laid by Schlüter. Besides the impact of his own methodological and substantive work, Schlüter exerted his influence through the dissertations on settlement geography that he supervised at the University of Halle. The most notable of these for the development of urban morphology was that on Danzig by Geisler, published in 1918.[22] Investigating specific aspects of urban form in much greater detail than had been done before, this work also improved on the technique of presentation, being illustrated by photographs of buildings and containing a major map of inner Danzig at the scale of 1/10000, distinguishing in colour land and building utilization and the number of storeys in residential buildings.[23] Within six years it was followed by Geisler's major work in urban morphology, *Die deutsche Stadt*, an extensive comparative study of three morphological aspects culminating in comprehensive classifications of the sites, town plans and building types of German towns.[24] These two publications established Geisler as a central figure in urban morphology. Four years later, however, the subject of the descriptive classification of town plans had already become controversial in terms of purpose and substance when it was once again treated comprehensively, in Martiny's study of the plan formation of the settlements of Germany.[25]

These last two works in a way marked the culmination of the very active period of urban morphological research during the decade following the First World War, which has been reviewed by Dörries,[26] one of its most prominent participants.[27] Geisler's identification and description of urban house types, though somewhat generalized, represented a useful advance in urban morphology capable of further development. However, in their attempt at extensive treatment of town plans neither Geisler nor Martiny was by any means fully successful. By attempting these comprehensive surveys of town plans over the whole of Germany and unrelated to relevant advances in urban history and the history of town planning, Geisler and Martiny, so far from reflecting the creditable work already done on this aspect in local monographs, including their own, allowed themselves to be pushed by the enormous scope of their projects into merely morphographic classification, producing profuse nomenclature with little meaning. Thus, they aggravated a tendency towards mere morphography already apparent in the poorer types of settlement monographs. This unfortunate failure of purpose occurred in spite of Schlüter's clearly and repeatedly expressed concept of *Kulturgeographie* and Oberhummer's emphasis on the historico-geographical perspective.[28]

The origin of the morphographic approach to town plans can be traced back much earlier to a modestly presented essay on German "town layouts" by the Strassburg High School teacher Fritz.[29] Realizing the potential of the town plan as a historic source and impressed by the contrast between eastern and western Germany in the general style of medieval town plans, he suggested a broad division into "regular" and "irregular" layouts. He interpreted this as a contrast between younger "planned" and older "spontaneously grown" towns. Although subsequently this interpretation turned out to be quite wrong, the general idea of stock-taking based on map inspection stimulated Schlüter[30] and also the historian Meier,[31] who recognized four purely descriptive types of town plan. Similarly, Gradmann used an even simpler classification for south-west German town plans, consisting of spine-and-rib, ladder, and transitional forms.[32] Some of the dissertations on the settlement geography of smaller areas set great store by such classifications. However, for experienced practitioners in regional settlement geography like Schlüter or Gradmann[33] this kind of morphography was at best a convenience for quick review. It was of limited use unless it revealed characteristic variations of forms over large areas and thereby posed a research problem as it had done for Fritz.

Morphographic classification of urban street systems proved particularly weak in four respects. First, by confining itself to the examination of street systems as shown on simple small-scale street plans it was liable to overlook the essential period compositeness of town plans that was evident from the historical study of actual cases. Thus it deprived its classes of real meaning and at the same time was overwhelmed by the immense variability of street-system configuration, each case seeming to be strictly individual. Secondly, failure to consult large-scale topographical plans excluded the evidence of plan detail in street lines and plot boundaries, thereby precluding the recognition of those elusive growth seams that are crucial in the identification of genetic plan units. Thirdly, examination confined to the modern plan could not reveal slow piecemeal changes in the detail of a plan and might therefore lead to misinterpretation of the existing street pattern. Fourthly, failure to consider streets without their associated plot and building patterns seriously impeded the recognition of the functional differences between streets.

These limitations of plan morphography[34] applied whenever urban geographers worked in isolation from relevant advances in urban constitutional and economic history[35] and the history of town planning. Indeed, developments in these two subjects in the German-speaking countries are sufficiently important to the urban morphogenetic method to merit a brief discussion of their roles as interrelated strands in its development.

The interest of German urban historians in the topographical aspect of the origin and development of medieval towns goes back to the work of Rietschel, especially his important book on the legal relation between market and town.[36] On the basis of extensive work with urban diplomatic sources he discovered, contrary to common assumption, that the majority of older towns in Germany had not grown spontaneously from villages but were deliberately founded, and that their origin showed a characteristic dualism of a planned market settlement and an adjacent older nucleus, such as a castle, royal palace, bishop's seat, monastery or village, with which it coalesced in time. Although he himself was not specially concerned with the topographical aspect of this, his findings aroused the topographical interest of other historians of medieval towns. Faced with an incomplete diplomatic record posing serious problems of interpretation they came to realize the possibilities of the existing townscape as a historical document and so developed a new research method complementary to the established diplomatic method and eventually called "urban constitutional topography" (*städtische Verfassungstopographie*) by Frölich, one of its prominent practitioners.[37] This line of research began with the work of Meier in 1909.[38] It gathered momentum and broadened during the inter-war period, when a number of important studies, such as Rörig's work on the market of Lübeck and Hamm's on the town foundations of the Dukes of Zähringen, were published.[39] Thus topographically conscious urban historians were making discoveries of importance to urban geographers concerning the nature of the social forces responsible for the origin, development and physical build of medieval towns. Yet during much of the inter-war period many urban geographers took little notice of this fact, despite their interest in genetic urban morphology. Only in the later inter-war period did this situation begin to change for the better, when the best geographical monographs began to refer to relevant literature in urban history. An example is Scharlau's treatment of eight medieval towns in his monograph on the historical settlement geography of the Knüll District in Hessen.[40] He even reproduced cadastral town plans of the eighteenth century, showing streets, plots and block-plans of buildings, but his use of them for genetic analysis, though effective in substance, still lacked precision in detail. Subsequently work on the topographical aspects of urban history in central Europe has increased greatly as indicated by Keyser's bibliography of urban history in Germany.[41] It has been carried on in the context of a lively all-European discussion on the origin and development of the medieval town in Europe.[42] Its improvement of method in the use of the large-scale town plan as a historical document, often in combination with archaeological evidence, is indicated by the publications of Strahm and especially those of Keyser and Stoob.[43]

These developments in urban history impinged strongly from an early date on the work of central European architects interested in the history of town planning. The fact that their professional training produced early awareness and technical understanding of the significance of artefacts on the ground partly explains why architects were interested in the socio-economic context of medieval urban origins and development that urban historians were discovering. This interest was already evident early in the century in the introductory sections of the studies by Klaiber, Meurer and Siedler.[44] Klaiber's and Siedler's studies were contrasting and complementary in the sense that the former related principally to the historically older area of western Germany while the latter covered the Askanian marches of Brandenburg, lying astride the Rivers Elbe and Oder, a particularly interesting area of the medieval East German colonization. This area provides perhaps the best example of medieval town planning development within the great planning laboratory provided by that colonization, stretching as it does from the earliest stage west of the Elbe to the latest east of the Oder. Siedler recognized this and analysed the plan of every medieval town in the area, frequently finding period compositeness, but he did not map the distribution of medieval plan types. Nor, on the whole, did he use plot patterns for the identification of genetic plan units. However, in his classification of plan types on the basis of the functional differentiation of streets and in his comparative study of approximately 150 town plans, Siedler's work was a significant methodological advance and set a high standard among his professional colleagues. The interest in medieval town planning among architects in central Europe has been sustained ever since.[45]

The fact that until the middle inter-war years research by architects on the history of town planning remained, like the work of urban historians, largely unknown to German urban geographers had a stultifying effect on plan morphology. In addition there was the problem that urban geography itself had not yet produced a sufficiently coherent body of knowledge about the social and economic organization of towns to make a more penetrating urban morphology possible. It is not surprising therefore that Geisler's and Martiny's elaborate classification schemes, overstretched in scope relative to the available sources of information, aroused criticism for tending to be ends in themselves and of marginal value to the development of urban geography and for that matter of related fields, such as historical geography, shared with other disciplines. In the ensuing controversy these extensive schemes and their cumbersome nomenclature soon came to be known facetiously as *erschöpfend* in its double sense, the German word meaning both "exhaustive" and "exhausting".[46] Critical comments to the same effect were made by the historian Vogel who had a long-standing interest in historical geography.[47] But much the most important criticism came from Bobek in his famous clarion call to urban geographers on fundamental problems of urban geography.[48] Writing this paper at the age of 23, fresh from the experience of his dissertation on Innsbruck[49] and seven years before the appearance of Christaller's work on the central places in southern Germany,[50] Bobek recognized the justification for Schlüter's main programmatic point of 1899[51] and acknowledged the geographical merit and progress of the morphological school. But he rightly pointed to the illogicality of concentrating attention on the forms in the urban landscape at the expense of the dynamic source that created these forms, which he saw in "the role of the town as a living economic organ within the economic system of the region".[52] He emphasized the pressing need for the investigation of this role and in opposition to Geisler's and Dörries's morphological formulations redefined the town from a geographical standpoint as "a larger settlement representing the universal economic, political and cultural communication centre of an indistinctly bounded area and having a physical build the characteristic features of which tend to intensify towards the centre".[53] This cautious definition therefore included the form of the town. It is also interesting that his elaboration of this and his subsequent discussion of the way in which urban economics is conditioned geographically are repeatedly illustrated by historical comparisons.[54] Thus already in his first methodological paper, and unlike some later American critics of urban morphology, Bobek was fully aware of the essential trinity of fundamental aspects attaching to the geographical nature of towns, as of other objects on the earth's surface, namely function, form, and change through time. However, the fact of this wide and receptive philosophical view, which is also evident in all his subsequent methodological and substantive work, and the fact that with this paper he initiated functional urban geography in central Europe was to be overshadowed by the impact created when Christaller, with a much narrower but sharply focused vision, took up one aspect of Bobek's idea and so presented urban geography with perhaps its most potent functional research model.[55] It was this and the flaws in the development of urban morphology already described that was ultimately to bring about a major change of course in the mainstream of urban geography during and at the end of the Second World War, involving the relegation of urban morphology to a comparatively minor role.

Conzen's early years in geography and planning[56]

Conzen began his training in the Geographical Institute in the University of Berlin in 1926, one year before the retirement of Albrecht Penck and at a time of increasing intellectual ferment in urban geography. Already a generally sympathetic environment for settlement studies existed well beyond the universities. Some of the earlier academic work on settlements produced in disciplines such as geography, history and architecture had filtered through to the schools and the general public in a variety of publications. The comparatively early and sustained interest within the German-speaking countries in the town as a physical entity should be viewed in this light. For example, illustrations of the historical growth and geographical aspects of villages and towns figured prominently in progressive school geography textbooks of the Weimar Republic, such as those of Fischer and Geistbeck, usually in the form of excerpts from small- and medium-scale topographical maps. A tradition of providing thematic maps on settlements in school and general atlases[57] and in historical atlases[58] also began after the First World War. Thus basic information on settlement types and distributions was widely available before investigations had begun in English-speaking countries and where indeed such information is still largely lacking today—in Britain for example there is not even an elementary knowledge of the national distribution of different types of medieval urban street systems.

A further general consideration, and one that is germane both to an understanding of Conzen's intellectual development and to an explanation of the fundamental nature of the contributions to urban morphology that emanated from central Europe during the first four decades of this century, is the breadth of perspective that German-speaking geographers were capable of bringing to bear on their research. Bobek, for example, whose study of Innsbruck, published in 1928, would not have seemed conceptually out of date if it had appeared 30 years later in the English-language literature,[59] also undertook extensive research in geomorphology, ecology and the geography of agriculture.[60] This was not an eclecticism stemming from an original training in another discipline, for unlike in English-speaking countries it was already in the 1920s normal for young geographers in central Europe to have undergone a university training in geography; rather it was a more integrated view of the discipline than was prevalent in Britain and America. Thus it was not an anachronism that Louis, a contemporary and colleague of Bobek in the Geographical Institute in the University of Berlin in the early 1930s and now with a long-established international reputation as a geomorphologist, should have published a paper in 1936 on the geographical structure of Greater Berlin.[61] What is perhaps remarkable is that in that paper he should have sown the seeds of what Openshaw has suggested[62] may be the most important development in urban morphology so far. For in Louis's *Stadtrandzonen* we have the first recognition of the urban fringe belts that a quarter of a century later were, in a conceptually much more developed form, to play a major part in Conzen's structuring of the morphological evolution of the English market town of Alnwick.[63] Conzen attended the lectures and field seminars of, among others, Penck, Krebs, Troll, Louis and Bobek, and was thus able to experience the full intellectual vigour that characterized the Geographical Institute in Berlin at its zenith.

Among the special advantages of the Institute were an academic staff of unrivalled diversity and quality, virtually all of whom had already made or were later to make major contributions to the advancement of geography, a corresponding diversity of postgraduate work and, not least, the highly-prized privilege for advanced students of attending colloquia at which new research was subjected to critical discussion by authorities inside and outside the Institute. The key features of the training offered may be summarized under five heads: first, intensive and accurate observation of geographical phenomena both in the field and on maps; secondly, the search for the processes producing such phenomena and the underlying forces involved; thirdly, unambiguous conceptualization of observed phenomena on the basis of these processes and forces and in readiness for testing and improvement by comparative study; fourthly, the devising of an appropriate cartographic expression for concepts formed; and finally, the maintenance of an interdisciplinary perspective on any geographical problem.

In this general context and with the possibility of seeing graduate students at work on many different aspects, Conzen soon came to acquire a special interest in Schlüter's original morphological approach to *Kulturgeographie*, the analogy in geomorphology, particularly in terms of the search for processes and the forces underlying them, having been well demonstrated to him by Louis's research excursions. He became interested in the morphology of the cultural landscape, increasingly concentrating his attention on settlements[64] and ultimately on towns,[65] stimulated in particular by Bobek's field seminars. Attendance at the seminars in historical geography held jointly by the historian Vogel, the local economic historian Hoppe and the geologist Solger ensured an interdisciplinary perspective. This intellectual inheritance was fundamental to the type of urban morphology that Conzen was later to introduce into Britain and which in the more recent post-war years has begun to give rise to a sizable literature in the English language.

Conzen's emigration in 1933 meant a sudden interruption to his career in geography and a delay of nearly 10 years before he could resume it. In the interval he trained for a career in town and country planning at the University of Manchester, leading to a spell of four years of work as a practising planner in a fairly extensive and very diversified area in north-west England. Having responsibility for the varied day-to-day work of a planning consultant's office and being in charge of a planning staff of from eight to twelve people, he had the opportunity to experience at first hand the great change of settlement pattern and its underlying social and economic forces in an area stretching from the industrial and residential east and south sides of the east-Lancashire conurbation to the specialized dairy farming area of south-west Cheshire and from there to the gates of Chester. The planning treatment of the continuous stream of building applications for that area had to be dealt with or supervised by him, but his interest in theoretical questions that had been stimulated in Berlin was by no means lost and he was much concerned with what was to him an appalling lack of any coherent conceptual or theoretical foundation for planning at that time. He made an attempt to devise a framework for the organization of planning science[66] which exhibits his concern for concept formulation and the systematization of relationships, both characteristics reflected at a more obvious level in the quest for terminological precision, that stemmed naturally from his training in Berlin.

Although Conzen had no opportunity for geographical research during that busy "planning" period, he was at least able to keep in touch with the current British and international geographical literature through the library of the Geographical Association then at Manchester under Fleure, who had followed and indeed actively supported his progress ever since 1933. When the Second World War brought town and country planning to a halt, Conzen was called back to Manchester University for simultaneous part-time work in the temporary Research Group on Rural Planning, set up by R. A. Cordingley, and in the Department of Geography. For the former his work included the translation of excerpts from Christaller's book on the central places of southern Germany, in the latter he held a temporary lecturing appointment whilst simultaneously preparing his M.A. thesis on the early historical geography of Chester under the supervision of Fleure. During that time he wrote a paper on the historical geography of East Prussia with emphasis on the medieval German colonization and later changes.[67] The sensitivity to topographical detail and particularly to the historical layering in the landscape that were brought together in an integrated cartographic expression in this paper were to become hallmarks of his work. Particular methodological interest attaches to the map showing the progress of German colonization by means of what he termed "isostades" (lines of equal stage).

During this period Conzen also began to familiarize himself with the form of the British town by a series of standardized reconnaissance surveys of individual towns small enough to enable him to carry out complete plot-by-plot surveys single-handed in one or two days. In each case the record comprised land and building utilization, building type of the plot dominant or dominants, building materials of walls, building materials of roofs, and floor-space concentration (number of storeys). The results for each town were represented on five maps, four of them polychrome and one monochrome, on the Ordnance Survey outline at the scale of 1/2500. The towns surveyed during the war were Frodsham, Conway and Ludlow, to be followed during the late 1940s by Newton Stewart, Wigtown, Whithorn, and Pickering. Some of this map material has been incorporated in monochrome form in later publications, but most of it has never been published, its main purpose having been to provide Conzen with a comparative view of basic aspects of the form of British towns.

The early post-war period

After the war Conzen moved to the Geography Department at King's College, Newcastle (later to become the University of Newcastle upon Tyne) where, apart from visiting appointments abroad, he was to spend the rest of his professional career. Not only did most of his subsequent work emanate from here but the surrounding area became his laboratory. In 1949 he published in association with a paper on settlements in north-eastern England[68] a map of settlement types over the whole of that region, showing symbolically the complete range of morphological types from isolated farmsteads to subdivisions of urban areas (involving several thousand settlements all together) classified by form and period characteristics. This has been without parallel in the English-speaking world. Its direct antecedent is Conzen's *Staatsexamen* map of 1931.[69] In the same year that it was published the morphogenetic tenets that underlay this map were combined with the methodological interest, that had already been evident in his earlier contribution on town planning, in a paper on the Scandinavian approach to urban geography.[70] This drew attention to the strength in Scandinavian countries of geographical research on the functional aspects of towns compared with the paucity of morphological studies, a situation, it was suggested, that might be interpreted as an understandable reaction against the limitations of the purely morphographic (as distinct from morphogenetic) approach to towns.

Conzen's continuing interest in the link between geography and planning in the 1950s was reflected in his *Geographie und Landesplanung in England*[71] but received its most developed expression in *A Survey of Whitby* in which he made a major contribution to an investigation that was undertaken in order to provide a basis for an integrated plan for the town of Whitby in east Yorkshire.[72] The result was both a unique record of the building types and land and building utilization of a whole town[73] and a demonstration of how a detailed elucidation of a town's morphological development can form the basis for townscape conservation.

Key features of the Whitby study are two large maps, one of building types and the other of land and building utilization, in which a number of cartographic innovations were made possible by the rare opportunity of being able to print in six colours at the large scale of 1/2609 (sheet size 127 cm × 97 cm).[74] The method of cartographic design used was a development from Conzen's reconnaissance surveys of the 1940s. It involved in the case of Whitby the recognition of 48 types of land and building utilization and 59 building types. The latter were defined on the basis of a combination of original function and period of origin, the second of these two criteria involving the assignment of buildings to one of five significant periods of social and economic history, which were thus different in principle, though not necessarily in practice, from periods based purely on architectural style such as were employed in Hassinger and Schaefer's early "art geography".[75] Individual types of buildings and of land and building utilization were grouped into larger classes which were assigned colours, as were the five period categories in the case of the building types. Within these larger classes individual types were distinguished by different line or dot patterns of a grain fine enough to allow them to be accommodated legibly within individual plots or building block-plans. An advantage of this method is that one and the same map can be viewed intelligibly at more than one reading distance. In this case a desk reading distance affords survey detail at the level of each plot and a distance of 1 m or more is effective for a synoptic reading of the whole map or its parts. Thus to some extent visual regionalizations become possible at different levels of resolution.

These two large maps of Whitby were a great advance on the much earlier ones produced by Hassinger[76] and Geisler.[77] For subsequent work that is at all comparable in terms of its morphological purpose we must look again to central

Europe, notably to Bobek and Lichtenberger's massive and seminal study of Vienna with its increased sophistication of presentation appropriate to its much larger and more famous subject.[78]

The study of Whitby is at once an important contribution to both urban morphology and applied geography. It suggests a number of bases for a townscape conservation strategy, pride of place being given to the role of the townscape in providing a community with a sense of continuity. In Conzen's words, the townscape

> "is an educational asset capable of introducing the younger generation into the life of its own community by one of the most impressive methods, the visual one. It puts the present generation and its work into an historic context and in the material residue left in the townscape by the labours of the past, provides object lessons in achievements as well as in failures. Thereby it helps to create a sense of that humanity which cares for the efforts of others and has a thought for future generations when shaping its own work."[79]

It is salutary to realize that this statement immediately pre-dated the main wave of post-war central redevelopment in British towns and cities that was to damage irreparably a major part of that country's townscape heritage. The perceptions that Conzen provides in the Whitby study on the townscape as an asset to future generations are developed further in two later papers reproduced in this volume (Chapters 3 and 4).

In spite of Conzen's work the mood in urban morphology in the 1950s outside the German-speaking countries was not conducive to a thorough-going morpho-genetic approach. In America urban morphology scarcely existed as a research field, except in the form of land-use studies. The cultural geography of the Berkeley school, though having had its earlier manifestations in the work of such scholars as Leighly,[80] Spencer[81] and Stanislawski,[82] was generally more productive in its application to rural than to urban landscapes.[83] In Britain a concern with the descriptive classification of existing townscapes,[84] albeit accompanied by some historical context, tended to hold sway over thorough-going evolutionary studies, at least of a type that attempted to conceptualize mor-phological developments.

Against this background Conzen worked during much of the 1950s on a study that was to prove itself the major contribution to urban morphology in the English language in the post-war era. This was *Alnwick, Northumberland: a study in town-plan analysis*.[85] Its achievements may be summarized under five heads: first, the establishment of a basic framework of principles for urban morphology; secondly, the adoption for the first time in the geographical literature in the English language of a thorough-going evolutionary approach; thirdly, the recognition of the individual plot as being the fundamental unit of analysis; fourthly, the use of detailed cartographic analysis (especially employing large-scale plans) in conjunction with field survey and documentary evidence; and fifthly, the conceptualization of developments in the townscape. The German academic tradition from which the study springs is manifest in each one of these respects, yet in what is achieved the study goes far beyond any previous investigations in this field in German or any other language. Its connection with the previous academic literature in the English language is small, much less than a casual scrutiny of its bibliography might suggest.

The tripartite division of the townscape into town plan, building forms and land use that was recognized in the Alnwick study has since become widely accepted. In fact *Alnwick* was only concerned with the town plan although it was originally conceived as the first of a trilogy of volumes that together would cover the complete morphological development of a single urban area. The volume on the town plan, to which Conzen gave priority on the grounds that the town plan "forms the inescapable framework for the other man-made features and provides the physical link between these on the the one hand and the physical site as well as the town's past existence on the other",[86] proved to be a massive undertaking in itself and the other two volumes have not been completed, although a manuscript map of the building fabric has existed for some time. The subdivision of the town plan for analytical purposes into streets and their arrangement in a street system, plots and their aggregation in street-blocks, and buildings, or more precisely their block-plans, has become a further standard way of reducing the complexity of reality to more manageable proportions.

In discussing his approach in the Alnwick study Conzen writes: "An evolutionary approach, tracing existing forms back to the underlying formative processes and interpreting them accordingly, would seem to provide the rational method of analysis."[87] The "retrogressive" method of working back from present-day forms is rejected quite simply because a proper understanding of processes cannot be attained from the analysis of relics, even in the case of the town plan, which produces a more complete collection of residual features than the building fabric or the land-use pattern: those parts of the townscape that have been removed are as important to a theory of townscape development as those that have survived. Thus the morphographic approach of classifying present-day survivals is rejected, although for the urban archaeologist these may be all that is available. Instead evolutionary patterns are assembled by utilizing such sources as rentals, building plans submitted in connection with applications to build, and large-scale printed and manuscript plans for past periods, in association with detailed plot-by-plot and building-by-building field surveys that include the recording of detailed topographical information on large-scale Ordnance Survey plans.

There was no direct precursor of Conzen's evolutionary approach to town-plan analysis, least of all in the English-language literature which had remained at the largely morphographic level exemplified by Dickinson's study of the town plans of East Anglia.[88] The recognition of the importance of plots, however, and of their role in the internal space organization of medieval towns is found in several earlier German-language studies, notably Strahm's study of the medieval town plan of Bern,[89] and a concern for plot dimensions was evident in the much earlier work of Siedler.[90]

Conzen's frequency analysis of the frontage widths of burgages (the plots held by the enfranchised members of a medieval borough) enabled him to draw a number of inferences about original burgage dimensions in Alnwick and to advance the thesis that in the oldest part of the borough there may have been a standard burgage frontage of 28–32 feet, probably conditioned by the use of a building unit consisting of two structural bays. For the detail of cartographic analysis underlying this and other aspects, such as street lines, there is again no direct antecedent.[91] The study by Keyser is highly sensitive to the plot structure of the town plan (but not the building block-plans), in notable contrast to the lack of any such interest by English-speaking historians, but when this was published the work on Alnwick was largely complete[92] and in any case the wide coverage of towns attempted by Keyser precluded the depth of treatment that characterized the study of Alnwick. Using successive large-scale plans for later periods and borough surveys for earlier ones, Conzen was able to piece together much of the evolution of the pattern of burgages from the mid-sixteenth century onward and, paying especial attention to the seams separating plot series of different genetic types, he arrived at a delimitation of plan units. In Conzen's own words:

> "Examination of the town plan shows that the three element complexes of streets, plots and buildings enter into individualized combinations in different areas of the town. Each combination derives uniqueness from its site circumstances and establishes a measure of morphological homogeneity or unity in some or all respects over its area. It represents a plan-unit, distinct from its neighbours."[93]

The resultant elucidation of the town plan had a subtlety far beyond anything previously conceived.

A major structuring device that takes on a more explicit role in the Alnwick study, though employed earlier by Conzen, is the morphological period, namely a phase of social and cultural history creating distinctive material forms in the cultural landscape. It is not, it should be stressed, just a device for separating older and younger areas determined by the incidence of cartographic records.[94] Furthermore, the changes that the town plan undergoes through successive morphological periods can rarely if ever be understood as unconstrained additions or replacements. An existing plan feature frequently exerts an influence on subsequent development, constituting a morphological frame in contact with which a subsequent plan unit develops more or less comfortably.

Conzen's conceptualizations of aspects of the development of the town plan have a variety of derivations. Occasionally a concept, or a term used to describe it, can be related fairly directly to earlier German studies. This is the case with the term "urban fallow", used to describe the temporary urban wasteland caused by socio-economic changes leading to building clearance, which is derived from Hartke's *Sozialbrache* or social fallow, a term applied, by analogy to the fallow in agricultural rotation, to rural field or vineyard land lying partly or wholly waste while the owner works elsewhere.[95] But others, such as the burgage cycle, are new conceptions. This cycle, consisting of the progressive filling-in with buildings of the backland of burgages and terminating in the clearing of buildings and a period of urban fallow prior to the initiation of a redevelopment cycle, is a particular variant of a more general phenomenon of building repletion where plots are subject to increasing pressure, often associated with changed functional requirements, in a growing urban area. Such a developmental concept is, of course, consistent with the German research tradition in which Conzen grew up, and it is a little paradoxical that Möller, an accomplished German urban morphologist,[96] should in her detailed and appreciative review of *Alnwick*[97] see in the use of the word "cycle" a suggestion of recurrence and therefore the influence of a supposedly "simplifying biologistic approach characteristic of Anglo-Saxon settlement geography". Conzen, well aware of the non-recurrence of the burgage cycle, though of course he envisaged the possibility of many redevelopment cycles, employed the word "cycle" in the more general sense of "a round, course or period through which anything runs to its completion".[98]

The fringe-belt concept as conceived in *Alnwick* represents a major development of Louis's *Stadtrandzone*[99]: indeed it may be viewed as the most important construct in Conzen's conception of a developing urban area. Put simply, urban fringe belts are the physical manifestations of periods of slow movement or actual standstill in the outward extension of the built-up area and characterized in the initial stages of their development by a variety of extensive users of land, such as various kinds of institutions, public utilities and country houses, usually with below average accessibility requirements to the main part of the built-up area. In Alnwick three such belts were recognized (inner, intermediate and outer fringe belts) at varying distances from the town centre. An important aspect both in Alnwick and more generally is the role of fixation lines, such as town walls, marking major limitations on the outward growth of the built-up area and heavily conditioning the pattern of subsequent growth. Particularly noteworthy in terms of the development of Louis's original notion is the recognition of a distinction in the case of a fringe belt associated with a town wall, or similar sharply-defined limitation to growth, between the restricted intramural zone, consisting mainly of secondary development within the generally close-grained morphological frame of a traditional plot pattern, and the extramural zone, consisting of more open, sometimes dispersed, development associated with the greater topographical freedom afforded by the relatively large-grained rural field pattern. Developments taking place following the creation of a fringe belt, notably the way in which the belt is perpetuated in spite of being encompassed by the built-up area but also the absorption of certain of its plots by advancing residential accretions, are also examined.

Despite the large amount of previous work by German-speaking scholars, and by this time English-speaking scholars too, there is no doubt that in the Alnwick study there is a depth of treatment without an earlier parallel. In its recognition of recurrent processes and formulation of a technical language for comparative work it stands in contrast to contemporary work by British historical geographers[100] and the few British historians concerned with the landscape.[101] It was a major breakthrough in the theoretical development of urban morphology. The concepts it produced can justifiably claim a significance in morphological analysis well beyond the particular case considered: the foundations had been laid for comparative studies and a major turning point had been reached in the history of research on the urban landscape.

Conzen's contributions since 1960

The appearance of the Whitby Survey and the study of Alnwick within the space of two years set new standards for urban morphological research in Britain. Not only had the Whitby Survey contained the first detailed geographical survey of the building fabric in the English-language literature but it had drawn attention to the implications of the processes affecting that fabric for townscape conservation. The Alnwick study had highlighted the complexity of the town plan, revealing, for example, the limitations of simple categorizations such as "planned" and "unplanned" towns and emphasizing the intimate relation between plan and site:[102] henceforth plots were to be almost a *sine qua non* of geographical town-plan analysis. Together these two works provided the main stepping-stones from which Conzen's subsequent publications have sprung.

A basic tenet of Conzen's papers of the 1960s and 1970s, four of which comprise Chapters 2–5, is that any form element or group of elements is essentially determined by two criteria. These are original function and period of origin, it being axiomatic that it is the social and economic conditions of particular historical periods that are crucial, as distinct from the age of forms measured in number of years or, indeed, purely architectural-style periods as employed by Hassinger in Vienna.[103] Period typologies must be grounded in time spans that have a degree of unity within the course of social and economic history: those based on arithmetic divisions or reflecting only the availability of source materials are liable to obscure rather than aid explanation. The adoption of this view coupled with minute attention to topographical detail is basic to Conzen's unravelling of the complexities of urban morphological structure. It is instrumental, for example, in bringing to light the highly composite nature of British town plans:[104] Keyser's plans of medieval towns in north-west Germany also revealed this composite-ness,[105] and it has recently been further demonstrated in German town-plan atlases.[106]

The conceptualization of developments in the landscape that was such a salient feature of the Alnwick study is even more prominent in the study of central Newcastle (Chapter 2) published two years later, in 1962.[107] This to a considerable extent builds on the conceptual groundwork undertaken in Alnwick. The more vigorous and functionally diversified development of a major city provides an opportunity for the wider applications of the method employed in Alnwick and for the examination of more developed varieties of the processes identified there. The process of plot metamorphosis in a complex city centre is traced in detail and conceptualized. The fringe-belt concept is further elaborated, notably in terms of the concepts of expansion, consolidation and functional segregation. As in Alnwick, Conzen eschews explanations in terms of specific economic or social mechanisms, not because he believes that they are unimportant but rather because he feels that past neglect of the actual physical processes establishes at least some temporary priority for the investigation of these.

The plan units that are identified are the products of these processes and are crucial not only for elucidation of the town plan but also, as becomes clear in the papers on applied townscape analysis published in 1966 and 1975 (Chapters 3 and 4), in the search for a theoretical basis for townscape conservation. The recognition of plan units depends on the detailed examination in genetic terms of street and building lines, building block-plans, and the shape, size, orientation and grouping of plots. As in Alnwick, such evidence provides a basis for recognizing the seams along which genetically significant plan units are knit together.[108] But plan units are only part of the townscape. As was evident in the Whitby Survey, the building fabric and the pattern of land and building utilization can be examined in a similar way and units mapped. If these are viewed in relation to one another and to the plan units, morphological regions can be recognized (Chapter 4, Fig. 1). This is done by superimposing on one another the three delimitations of areal subdivisions in order to arrive at a composite regionalization. It is an approach that has its antecedence in extensive discussions among German-speaking geographers on the theory of regionalization, but these discussions have not been specifically concerned with the internal morphological divisions of the town and investigation of this particular subject is only in its initial stages. The method that Conzen uses in his reconnaissance of the problem, namely deriving a hierarchy of morphological divisions from the degree of boundary coincidence between the three basic form complexes of the townscape, is the same in principle as that employed by Granö in his experiment on a much larger regional scale.[109] However, the results are quite different. Granö was left at the end with a large number of more or less uniformly small regions, in some cases with inordinately wide boundary belts between them, that did not nest into any meaningful hierarchy. In contrast Conzen's experiment was bound to exhibit the general sharpness of boundaries inherent in the very nature of the townscape and to produce a clear hierarchy of such boundaries with a direct relation to the historical provenance of the town and its present functional structure.

As Conzen makes clear in Chapter 4, however, there is still no comprehensive theory of urban form capable of providing a basis for application to planning practice. Studies of townscape conservation have inevitably lacked penetration without a substructure of townscape-development theory. But the papers that comprise Chapters 3 and 4 go some way towards developing a conception of the townscape in which the recognition of morphological regions according to academic criteria becomes a practical device for establishing guide lines for townscape management. Fundamental to this perspective is the concept of the "objectivation of the spirit". In geography this philosophical concept appears first in the work of the German geographer Schwind,[110] and goes back to studies on the philosophy of culture by German philosophers such as Freyer and Spranger.[111] In the present context it relates to the fact that urban landscapes embody not only the efforts and aspirations of the people occupying them at present but also those of their predecessors: they are conditioned by culture and history. This enables individuals and groups to take root in an area. They acquire a sense of the historical dimension of human experience, which stimulates comparison and encourages a less time-bound and more integrated approach to contemporary problems. Landscapes with a high degree of expressiveness of past societies exert a particularly strong educative and regenerative influence in this way. The fact that this is often experienced unconsciously and that it is not susceptible to direct measurement in terms of economic benefits does not lessen its importance. Thus to Conzen historical townscapes are important to society not only aesthetically but both intellectually and as a wider emotional experience. It is in his consideration of the intellectual benefits of the objectivation of the spirit and how the historical expressiveness of the landscape may be assessed that his practical contribution is particularly important: these two aspects constitute fundamental prerequisites for a proper strategy for townscape conservation. It is here that morphological regions can provide a link between morphological concepts and planning practice.

Conzen's contributions have tended to be strewn widely and inaccessibly, and it has been difficult for scholars to gather them together. Chapter 5 is a first attempt in English to synthesize his ideas about the urban landscape and the additive and transformative processes that create it, being essentially a translation from the German of his most recent paper published in 1978. Although it is not a completely rounded treatment of his work, it is the closest approximation so far available. Combined with Chapter 4 it provides us with a practically up-to-date statement of his field of view and a synoptic vantage point from which to approach the various attempts to build on his work that are discussed in Chapter 6.

Notes

1. For a different approach to urban morphogenesis see Vance, J. E. (1977) *This scene of man: the role and structure of the city in the geography of western civilization* (New York).

2. Dickinson, R. E. (1942) "The development and distribution of the medieval German town: I. The West German lands", *Geography* 27, 9–21; Dickinson, R. E. (1942) "The development and distribution of the medieval German town: II. The eastern lands of German colonisation", *Geography* 27, 47–53; Dickinson, R. E. (1945) "The morphology of the medieval German town", *Geogrl Rev.* 35, 74–97; Dickinson, R. E. (1948) "The scope and status of urban geography: an assessment", *Land Econ.* 24, 221–38; Dickinson, R. E. (1951) *The west European city: a geographical interpretation* (London).

3. Blanchard, R. (1912) *Grenoble: étude de geographie urbaine* (Paris).

4. Fleure, H. J. (1920) "Some types of cities in temperate Europe", *Geogrl Rev.* 10, 357–74.

5. Leighly, J. B. (1928) "The towns of Mälardalen in Sweden: a study in urban

morphology", *Univ. Calif. Publs Geogr.* **3**, 1–134; Leighly, J. B. (1939) "The towns of medieval Livonia", *Univ. Calif. Publs Geogr.* **6**, 235–313.

6. Schlüter, O. (1899a) "Über den Grundriss der Städte", *Z. Ges. Erdk. Berl.* **34**, 446–62.

7. Schlüter, O. (1899b) "Bemerkungen zur Siedlungsgeographie", *Georg. Z.* **5**, 65–84.

8. Schlüter, O. (1903) *Die Siedlungen im nordöstlichen Thüringen: ein Beispiel für die Behandlung siedlungsgeographischer Fragen* (Berlin).

9. Schlüter, O. (1906) *Die Ziele der Geographie des Menschen* (Munich).

10. Schlüter, O. (1919) *Die Stellung der Geographie des Menschen in der erdkundlichen Wissenschaft* (Berlin).

11. On Schlüter's significance for the methodological development of geography see Lautensach, H. (1952) "Otto Schlüter's Bedeutung für die methodische Entwicklung der Geographie", *Pet. Geog. Mitt.* **96/4** (Schlüterheft), 219–31, reprinted in Storkebaum, W. (ed.) (1975) *Zum Gegenstand und zur Methode der Geographie* (Darmstadt) pp. 36–81.

12. Ratzel, F. (1882–99, 1891) *Anthropogeographie* 2 vols (Stuttgart).

13. Schlüter (1906) op. cit. p. 11 (note 9).

14. Von Richthofen, F. (1883) *Aufgaben und Methoden der heutigen Geographie* Inaugural Lecture (Berlin) p. 25.

15. Schlüter (1899b) op. cit. p. 67 (note 7). Schlüter (1906) op. cit. p. 28 (note 9).

16. This standpoint, though not specifically expressed in these modern terms, informs the whole of Schlüter's monograph on the settlements of North-eastern Thuringia, Schlüter (1903) op. cit. (note 8), and indeed all his subsequent methodological and substantive work.

17. Schlüter (1906) op. cit. p. 3 (note 9).

18. Schlüter (1899b) op. cit. (note 7).

19. Hassinger, H. (1912a) *Wiener Heimatschutz und Verkehrsfragen* (Vienna); Hassinger (1912b) *Kunsthistorischer Plan des 1. Bezirkes der Stadt Wien 1/10000* (Vienna); Hassinger, H. (1915a) *Kunsthistorischer Übersichtsplan von Wien 1/25000* (Vienna); Hassinger, H. (1915b) "Kartographische Aufnahme des Wiener Stadtbildes", *Mitt. geogr. Ges. Wien* **58**; Hassinger, H. (1916) *Kunsthistorischer Atlas von Wien* Österreichische Kunsttopographie 15 (Vienna), containing plans of the Old Town showing architectural styles at the scale of 1/3960.

20. Schaefer, G. (1928) *Kunstgeographische Siedlungslandschaften und Städtebilder: Studien im Gebiet zwischen Strassburg-Bern-Dijon-Freiburg i.Br.* (Basel).

21. Hassinger, H. (1927) "Basel: ein geographisches Städtebild", *Beitrage zur oberrheinischen Landeskunde* (Karlsruher Geographentag, Festschrift) 103–30.

22. Geisler, W. (1918) *Danzig: ein siedlungsgeographischer Versuch* (Danzig).

23. It is indicative of the isolation of English-speaking geographers from research being undertaken in the German-speaking countries that in his study of Danzig Davies, A. (1933) "A study in city morphology and historical geography", *Geography* **18**, 25–37 makes no reference to Geisler's monograph on that city.

24. Geisler, W. (1924) *Die deutsche Stadt: ein Beitrag zur Morphologie der Kulturlandschaft* (Stuttgart).

25. Martiny, R. (1928) "Die Grundrissgestaltung der deutschen Siedlungen", *Pet. Geog. Mitt.* Ergänzungsheft **197**.

26. Dörries, H. (1930) "Der gegenwärtige Stand der Stadtgeographie", *Pet. Geog.*

Mitt. Ergänzungsheft **209**, 310–25. See also Dörries, H. (1940) "Siedlungs- und Bevölkerungsgeographie (1908–38)", *Geogr. Jb.* **55**.

27. Dörries, H. (1925) *Die Städte im oberen Leinetal Göttingen, Northeim und Einbeck* (Göttingen); Dörries, H. (1929a) *Entstehung und Formenbildung der niedersächsischen Stadt* (Stuttgart); Dörries, H. (1929b) "Die Städte am Nordrand des Harzes", *Geogr. Z.* **35**.

28. Oberhummer, E. (1907) "Der Stadtplan, seine Entwicklung und geographische Bedeutung", *Verhandlungen des 16. deutschen Geographentag zur Nürnberg, 1907* (Berlin) pp. 66–101.

29. Fritz, J. (1894) "Deutsche Stadtanlangen", *Beilage zum Programm 520 des Lyzeums Strassburg* (Strassburg).

30. Schlüter (1899a) op. cit. (note 6).

31. Meier, P. J. (1907) "Die Grundrissbildungen der deutschen Städte des Mittelalters in ihrer Bedeutung für Denkmälerbeschreibung und Denkmalpflege", *Stenographischer Bericht des 8. Tages für Denkmalpflege Mannheim 1907.*

32. Gradmann, R. (1914) *Die Stadtischen Siedlungen des Königreichs Württemberg* (Stuttgart).

33. Gradmann, R. (1928) "Die Arbeitsweise der Siedlungsgeographie", *Z. bayer. Landesgesch.* **1**, p. 350, footnote.

34. See also Keyser, E. (1958) *Städtegründungen und Städtebau in Nordwestdeutschland im Mittelalter* (Remagen) pp. 28–29, who expresses much the same criticism.

35. Vogel, W. (1930) "Stand und Aufgaben der Historisch-geographischen Forschung in Deutschland", *Pet. Geog. Mitt.* Ergänzungsheft **209** (Wagner Gedächtnisschrift) p. 353.

36. Rietschel, S. (1897) *Markt und Stadt in ihrem rechtlichen Verhältnis: ein Beitrag zur Geschichte der deutschen Stadtverfassung* (Halle), reprinted 1965 (Aalen); Ennen, E. (1953) *Frühgeschichte der europäischen Stadt* (Bonn) pp. 121–2; Frölich, K. (1953) "Das verfassungstopographische Bild der mittelalterlichen Stadt im Lichte der neueren Forschung", in von Brandt, A. and Koppe, W. (eds) *Städtewesen und Bürgertum als geschichtliche Kräfte* (Lübeck) p. 61.

37. Major methodological and atlas references in chronological order are Meier, P. J. (1909) "Der Grundriss der deutschen Stadt des Mittelalters in seiner Bedeutung als geschichtliche Quelle", *KorrespBl. Gesamtver. dt. Gesch. Altertumsver.* **57**, cols 105–21; Müller, K. O. (1912) *Die oberschwäbischen Reichsstädte ihre Entstehung und ältere Verfassung* (Stuttgart); Müller, K. O. (1914) *Alte und neue Stadtpläne der oberschwäbischen Reichsstädte* (Stuttgart); Meier, P. J. (1914) "Die Fortschritte in der Frage der Anfänge und der Grundrissbildung der deutschen Stadt", *KorrespBl. Gesamtver. dt. Gesch. Altertumsver.* **62**, cols 222–46; Meier, P. J. (1926–33 ff.) *Niedersächsischer Städteatlas* 1. Abt. Die braunschweigischen Städte, 2nd edn (Hanover) 1926, 2. Abt. Einzelne Städte, 1933–35, 1953, 3. Abt. Oldenburg, 1959; Uhlemann, W. (1931) "Stand und Aufgaben der Stadtplanforschung für die Geschichte des Städtewesens", *Vjschr. Soz. Wirtschgesch.* **24**, 185–212; Gerlach, W. (1935) "Alte und neue Wege der Stadtplanforschung", *Hansische Gesch. Bll.* **60**, 208–21; Frölich, K. (1938) "Zur Verfassungstopographie der deutschen Städte des Mittelalters", *Z. Savigny-Stift. Rechtsgesch.*, Germanistische Abt. **58**, 275–310; Strahm, H. (1950) "Zur Verfassungstopographie der mittelalterlichen Stadt mit besonderer Berücksichtigung des Gründungsplanes der Stadt Bern", *Z. Schweiz. Gesch.* **30**, 372–410; Frölich (1953) op. cit. 61–94 (note 36); Keyser, E. (1958) op. cit. (note 34). This last work is of special importance to the historical urban geographer because of the exhaustive demonstration of the use of plan detail in genetic plan analysis. See also Keyser,

E. (1969) *Bibliographie zur Städtegeschichte Deutschlands* (Cologne), a second edition of which is in preparation.

38. Meier, (1909, 1914, 1926–33 ff.) op. cit. (note 37).

39. Rörig, F. (1928) "Der Markt von Lübeck", *Hansische Beiträge zur deutschen Wirtschaftsgeschichte* (Breslau), reprinted in Rörig, F. (1959) *Wirtschaftskräfte im Mittelalter* (Cologne) pp. 36–133; Hamm, E. (1932) *Die Städtegründungen der Herzöge von Zähringen in Südwestdeutschland* (Freiburg i.B.).

40. Scharlau, K. (1941) *Siedlung und Landschaft im Knüllgebiet* (Leipzig).

41. Keyser (1969) op. cit. (note 37).

42. Ennen (1953) op. cit. (note 36); Ennen, E. (1972) *Die europäische Stadt des Mittelalters* (Göttingen).

43. Strahm, H. (1945) "Die Area in den Städten", *Schweizer Beitr. Allg. Gesch.* **3**, p. 40 ff.; Strahm, H. (1950) "Zur Verfassungstopographie der mittelalterlichen Stadt", *Z. Schweiz. Gesch.* **30**, pp. 406–7, 409–10; Keyser (1958) op. cit. (note 37); Stoob, H. (ed.) (1973) *Deutscher Städteatlas* vol. 1 (Dortmund); Stoob, H. (ed.) (1975) *Westfälischer Städteatlas* vol. 1 (Dortmund).

44. Klaiber, C. (1912) *Die Grundrissbildung der deutschen Stadt im Mittelalter* (Berlin); Meurer, F. (1914) *Der mittelalterliche Stadtgrundriss im nördlichen Deutschland* (Berlin); Siedler, E. J. (1914) *Märkischer Städtebau im Mittelalter* (Berlin).

45. Brinckmann, A. E. (1921) *Deutsche Stadtbaukunst in der Vergangenheit* (Frankfurt/M.); Hoenig, A. (1921) *Deutscher Städtebau in Böhmen* (Berlin); Gantner, J. (1928) *Grundformen der europäischen Stadt* (Vienna); Klaar, A. (1938) "Der mittelalterliche Städtebau in Österreich bis zum 13. Jahrhundert", in Ginhard, K. (ed.) (1937–38) *Die bildende Kunst in Österreich* (Vienna) vol. 2, pp. 82–9; Klaar, A. (1942) "Der mittelalterliche Wiener Stadtgrundriss", in Friedrich, W. (ed.) *Wien: die Geschichte einer deutschen Stadt an der Grenze* (Vienna) vol. 3; Klaar, A. (1948) "Die siedlungstechnischen Grundzüge der niederösterreichischen Stadt im Mittelalter", *Jb. Landesk. Niederöst. N.F.* **29**, 365–84; Klaar, A. (1957) "Die österreichische Stadt in ihrer geographischhistorischen Erscheinungsform", *Festschrift zur Jahrhundertfeier der Geographischen Gesellschaft* (Vienna); Klaar, A. (1963) "Die Siedlungsformen der österreichischen Donaustädte", in Rausch, W. (ed.) *Die Städte Mitteleuropas im 12. und 13. Jahrhundert* (Linz) pp. 93–115; Gruber, K. (1977) *Die Gestalt der deutschen Stadt* 3rd edn (Munich); Junghanns, K. (1959) *Die deutsche Stadt im Frühfeudalismus* (Berlin); Herzog, E. (1964) *Die ottonische Stadt* (Berlin).

46. Schöller, P. (1953) "Aufgaben und Probleme der Stadtgeographie", *Erdkunde* **7**, 161–84, reprinted in Schöller, P. (ed.) (1969) *Allgemeine Stadtgeographie* (Darmstadt) p. 56.

47. Vogel, W. (1926) Review of *Die deutsche Stadt*, *Dt. Literaturztg* 1926, col. 1298–1304.

48. Bobek, H. (1927) "Grundfragen der Stadtgeographie", *Geogr. Anz.* **28**, 213–24, reprinted in Schöller, op, cit. pp. 195–202 (note 46).

49. Bobek, H. (1928) *Innsbruck: eine Gebirgsstadt, ihr Lebensraum und ihre Erscheinung* (Stuttgart).

50. Christaller, W. (1933) *Die zentralen Orte in Süddeutschland* (Jena), reprinted (3rd edn) 1980 (Darmstadt).

51. Schlüter (1899b) op. cit. (note 7).

52. Bobek (1927) op. cit. p. 197 (note 48).

53. Ibid. p. 202.

54. Ibid. pp. 204–7, 212–13, 216–18.

55. Bobek's paper and its significance for urban geography has been largely ignored in the English-language literature. So has the fact that for a considerable time Christaller's work, especially his regional application in the second half of his book (largely omitted from the English translation), aroused fierce criticism in Germany from experienced regional geographers and delayed his recognition until after the Second World War.

56. Parts of this section and to a lesser extent subsequent sections in this chapter are based on biographical and related material that M. R. G. Conzen generously made available to the author. Where this is the case separate footnotes are not provided.

57. Haack, H. and Lautensach, H. (1931) *Sydow-Wagners Methodischer Schulatlas* 19th edn (Gotha); Diercke, C. and Dehmel, R. (1958) *Westermanns Hausatlas* (Braunschweig); Wenschow, K. (1948) *Heimat-Atlas Regierungsbezirk Schwaben* (Munich).

58. Stier, H.-E. *et al.* (1978) *Westermanns Grosser Atlas zur Weltgeschichte* (Braunschweig); Bayerischer Schulbuch-Verlag (1970) *Grosser Historischer Weltatlas, 2. Teil: Mittelalter* (Munich); Spindler, M. (1969) *Bayerischer Geschichtsatlas* (Munich).

59. Bobek (1928) op. cit. (note 49).

60. Dickinson, R. E. (1969) *The makers of modern geography* (London) pp. 167–8.

61. Louis, H. (1936) "Die geographische Gliederung von Gross-Berlin", *Länderkundliche Forschung* Krebs-Festschrift, 146–71.

62. Openshaw, S. (1974) "Processes in urban morphology with special reference to South Shields", unpubl. Ph.D. thesis, Univ. of Newcastle upon Tyne, p. 10.

63. Conzen, M. R. G. (1960) *Alnwick, Northumberland: a study in town-plan analysis* Inst. Br. Geogr. Publ. No. 27. A parallel but much better known example of a lengthy time-lag between the formulation of a concept in Germany and its assimilation into geography in the English-speaking world is central-place theory.

64. Conzen, M. R. G. (1931) "Ländliche und städtische Siedlungsgrundrisse in der Mark Brandenburg", unpubl. *Staatsexamen* map (with explanation, 26 pp.) MS map collection, Geogrl Inst., Univ. of Berlin. To avoid the ugly confusion of semi-descriptive and abstract symbols characterizing the maps of settlement types in the dissertations emanating from the Schlüter school at Halle, this 1/200 000 map was designed consistently on the principle that all settlements must be shown by standardized descriptive symbols so as to distinguish clearly between streets and associated built-up frontages as on medium-scale topographical maps.

65. Conzen, M. R. G. (1932) "Die Havelstädte", unpubl. *Staatsexamen* diss., Univ. of Berlin. This included field surveys of twelve small to medium-sized towns on the R. Havel (to the west and north of Berlin) which, using *inter alia* Geisler's urban house types, yielded maps of building types (scale 1/10 000) that provided a basis for the comparative analysis of the physical development of these towns.

66. Conzen, M. R. G. (1938) "Towards a systematic approach in planning science: geoproscopy", *Tn Plann. Rev.* **18**, 1–26.

67. Conzen, M. R. G. (1945) "East Prussia: some aspects of its historical geography", *Geography* **30**, 1–10.

68. Conzen, M. R. G. (1949a) "Modern settlement", in Isaac, P. C. G. and Allan, R. E. A. (eds) *Scientific survey of north-eastern England* (Newcastle upon Tyne) pp. 75–83.

69. Conzen (1931) op. cit. (note 64).

70. Conzen, M. R. G. (1949b) "The Scandinavian approach to urban geography", *Norsk. geogr. Tidsskr.* **12**, 86–91.

71. Conzen, M. R. G. (1952) *Geographie und Landesplanung in England* Colloquium Geographicum 2 (Bonn).

72. Conzen, M. R. G. (1958) "The growth and character of Whitby", in Daysh, G. H. J. (ed.) *A survey of Whitby and the surrounding area* (Eton) pp. 49–89.

73. Thurston undertook a wide-ranging morphological survey of St Albans in 1947–48 but chose to give comparatively little weight to his data on the building fabric in his subsequent published paper. See Thurston, H. S. (1953) "The urban regions of St Albans", *Trans. Inst. Br. Geogr.* **19**, 107–21.

74. This opportunity arose from the generosity of the originator, patron and copyright holder of the *Survey of Whitby*, the Marquis of Normanby who presented the Survey to Whitby Urban District Council.

75. Hassinger (1916) op. cit. (note 19); Schaefer, op. cit. (note 20).

76. Hassinger (1916) op. cit. (note 19).

77. Geisler (1918) op. cit. (note 22).

78. Bobek, H. and Lichtenberger, E. (1966) *Wien: Bauliche Gestalt und Entwicklung seit der Mitte des 19 Jahrhunderts* (Graz), especially the folded maps at the end. See also Lichtenberger, E. (1977) *Die Wiener Altstadt: von der mittelalterlichen Bürgerstadt zur City* (Vienna) Kartenband.

79. Conzen (1958) op. cit. p. 78 (note 72).

80. Leighly (1928) op. cit. (note 5).

81. Spencer, J. E. (1939) "Changing Chungking: the rebuilding of an old Chinese city", *Geogrl Rev.* **29**, 46–60.

82. Stanislawski, D. (1946) "The origin of the grid-pattern town", *Geogrl Rev.* **36**, 105–20.

83. For a similar view, see Conzen, M. P. (1978) "Analytical approaches to the urban landscape", *Univ. of Chicago Dep. Geogr. Res. Pap.* **186**, p. 130. See also Spencer, J. E. (1979) "A geographer west of the Sierra Nevada", *Ann. Ass. Am. Geogr.* **69**, p. 48.

84. For example, Smailes, A. E. (1955) "Some reflections on the geographical description and analysis of townscapes", *Trans. Inst. Br. Geogr.* **21**, 99–115; Smailes, A. E. and Simpson, G. (1958) "The changing face of East London", *East Lond. Pap.* **1**, 31–46; Stedman, M. B. (1958) "The townscape of Birmingham in 1956", *Trans. Inst. Br. Geogr.* **25**, 225–38; Jones, E. (1958) "The delimitation of some urban landscape features in Belfast", *Scott. geogr. Mag.* **74**, 150–62.

85. Conzen (1960) op. cit. (note 63).

86. Ibid. p. 4.

87. Ibid. p. 7.

88. Dickinson, R. E. (1934) "The town plans of East Anglia: a study in urban morphology", *Geography* **19**, 37–50.

89. Strahm, H. (1948) "Der zähringische Gründungsplan der Stadt Bern", *Arch. Hist. Ver. Kanton Bern.* **39**, 361–89.

90. Siedler, op. cit. p. 60 (note 44).

91. In contrast to the Alnwick study, cartographic analysis plays only a minor role in Strahm's study of Bern. Strahm (1950) op. cit. (note 43) contains only a small-scale reproduction of a "Bird's Eye View" and a single plan (p. 401), and Strahm (1948) op. cit. (note 89) lacks illustrative plans of any kind.

92. Keyser (1958) op. cit. (note 34).

93. Conzen (1960) op. cit. p. 5 (note 63).

94. For a subdivision of the urban landscape determined by the date for which map evidence was available, see Jones, op. cit. pp. 151–2 (note 84).

95. Hartke, W. (1953) "Die soziale Differenzierung der Agrarlandschaft im Rhein-Main-Gebiet", *Erdkunde* 7, 13–22; Hartke, W. (1956) "Die Sozialbrache als Phänomen der geographischen Differenzierung der Landschaft", *Erdkunde* 10, 257–69.

96. See, for example, Möller, I. (1959) *Die Entwicklung eines Hamburger Gebietes von der Agrar- zur Groszstadtlandschaft: mit einem Beitrag zur Methode der Städtischen Aufrissanalyse* Hamburger Geographische Studien 10 (Hamburg).

97. Möller, I. (1964) Review of *Alnwick Northumberland: a study in town-plan analysis*, *Pet. Geog. Mitt.*, **108**, 112–13.

98. Onions, C. T. (ed.) (1950) *The shorter Oxford English dictionary* (Oxford) p. 445.

99. Louis, op. cit. (note 61).

100. For example, Thorpe, H. (1950–51) "The city of Lichfield: a study of its growth and function", *Staffs. hist. Collect.*

101. For example, Hoskins, W. G. (1955) *The making of the English landscape* (London) esp. pp. 210–30; Beresford, M. (1957) *History on the ground* (London) esp. pp. 125–83.

102. See also Conzen, M. R. G. (1968) "The use of town plans in the study of urban history", in Dyos, H. J. (ed.) *The study of urban history* (London) p. 119.

103. Hassinger (1916) op. cit. (note 19).

104. Conzen (1968) op. cit. pp. 122–7 (note 102).

105. Keyser, op. cit. (note 34).

106. See, for example, Stoob (1973, 1975) op. cit. (note 43).

107. For an earlier study of Newcastle intended for a general readership see Conzen, M. R. G. (1949c) "Geographical setting of Newcastle", in Isaac and Allan, op. cit. pp. 191–7 (note 68).

108. See also Conzen (1968, op. cit. p. 120 (note 102).

109. Granö, J. G. (1929) "Reine Geographie: eine methodologische Studie beleuchtet mit Beispielen aus Finnland und Estland", *Acta geogr. Helsingf.* 2, 1–202.

110. Schwind, M. (1951) "Kulturlandschaft als objektivierter Geist", *Dte geogr. Bl.* **46**, 5–28; Schwind, M. (1964) *Kulturlandschaft als geformter Geist* (Darmstadt).

111. Freyer, H. (1934) *Theorie des objektiven Geistes: eine Einleitung in die Kulturphilosophie* 3rd edn (Leipzig) reprinted 1966 (Darmstadt); Spranger, E. (1936) *Probleme der Kulturmorphologie* Sonderausgabe aus dem Sitzungsbericht der Preussischen Akademie der Wissenschaften, Philosophisch-Historische Klasse (Berlin).

TWO

The plan analysis of an English city centre*

M. R. G. CONZEN

During the last 30 years, geographical work on the functional nature of towns has progressed considerably while that on urban morphology has lagged behind. Yet both these aspects are important since they contribute essentially to the character of the town as a geographical region. They are also interdependent. It seems appropriate, therefore, to look at the townscape afresh on the basis of our functional knowledge and with a more informed genetic approach.

Among the three aspects of the townscape accessible to direct observation, i.e. town plan, building types, and urban land use, the former is of fundamental importance in providing the basic framework. Recently, an evolutionary method of plan analysis has been developed in the study of an English market town.[1] Its concepts, covering recurrent phenomena in the old-established towns of Britain, appear to be of general significance and await the test of wider application. In this paper the method is applied to the complex case of an English city centre, central Newcastle upon Tyne.

It is useful to remember at the outset that geographically the town plan is a combination of three distinct but integral kinds of plan elements: the streets and their street system, the plots and their plot pattern, and the building arrangement within these patterns (Fig. 1).

The evidence

Newcastle upon Tyne is the regional capital of north-eastern England, a multi-functional town with a population in 1951 of 292 000 looking back on a development of more than 800 years.[2] It lies on the Tyne about halfway between the tidal limit of the estuary and the sea at a point where relatively resistant sandstones in the Coal Measures cause the coastal lowlands to rise above the surrounding area. The river has cut this undulating plateau in a narrow, steep-sided gorge some 800 feet below the edges, allowing high, dry land to

* First published in Norborg, K. (ed.) (1962) *Proceedings of the IGU symposium in urban geography Lund 1960* (Lund) pp. 383–414. Reprinted by permission of the Editor, *Lund Studies in Geography* Series B and C.

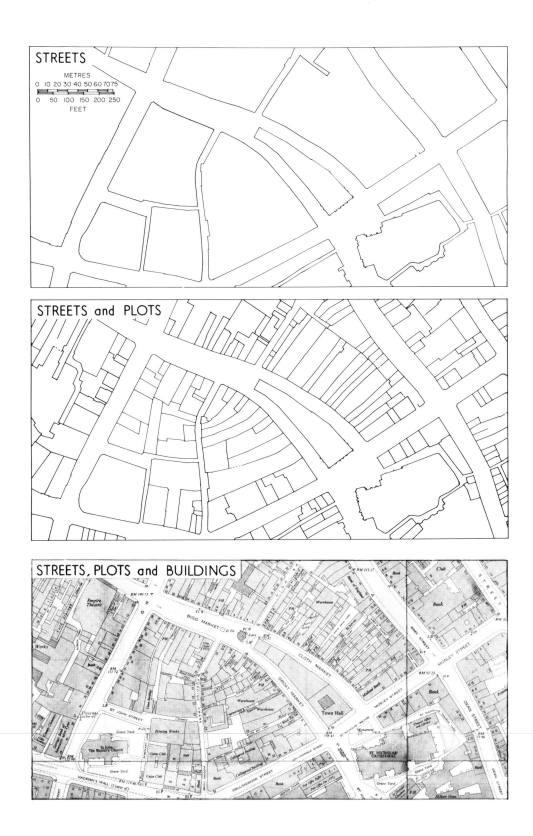

Figure 1. Elements of the town plan. Reproduced from the Ordnance Survey map with the permission of the Controller of Her Majesty's Stationery Office, Crown copyright reserved.

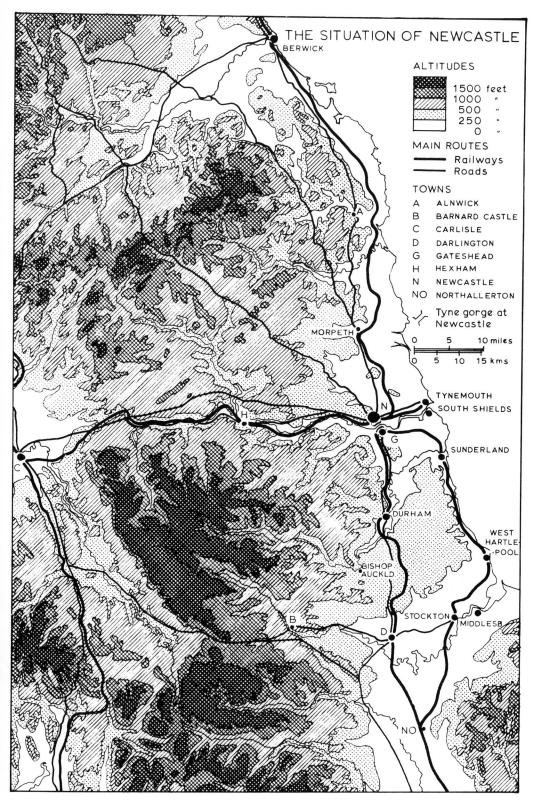

THE SITUATION OF NEWCASTLE

ALTITUDES

1500 feet
1000 "
500 "
250 "
0 "

MAIN ROUTES
———— Railways
———— Roads

TOWNS
A   ALNWICK
B   BARNARD CASTLE
C   CARLISLE
D   DARLINGTON
G   GATESHEAD
H   HEXHAM
N   NEWCASTLE
NO NORTHALLERTON

Tyne gorge at
Newcastle

0   5   10 miles
0 5 10 15 kms

BERWICK

A

MORPETH

H

C

N

TYNEMOUTH
SOUTH SHIELDS

G

SUNDERLAND

DURHAM

WEST
HARTLE-
-POOL

BISHOP
AUCKLD.

B

STOCKTON

D

MIDDLESB.

NO

Figure 2. The situation of Newcastle.

approach closely without the inconvenience of an intervening flood plain. These site circumstances have helped to make Newcastle the strategic river crossing and routeway centre of the North-east ever since its foundation (Fig. 2).

On the site of the old town the plateau margin is deeply dissected by streams or "burns" which at one time all reached their local base level by ravines locally known as "denes". Thus Lort Burn and Pandon Burn with their tributaries define a series of spurs of which the Castle Hill offered special advantages as the site of a strategic fortress (Fig. 3).

The important Norman castle was the pre-urban nucleus of the town and overlooked the new river bridge as well as the Great North Road which climbed the plateau through the dene immediately behind the Castle Hill (Fig. 4). The strategic situation soon proved to be of economic advantage and an open settlement of the suburbium type developed round the hill, with its market by the river and its church on the plateau.

The combined bridge point and estuarine seaport soon grew as an important borough trading in wool, leather and other merchandise and became the outstanding coal export centre of medieval England. Its built-up area spread along the river bank and over the three adjoining plateau interfluves so that the fourteenth-century town wall encompassed the pre-urban nucleus, the suburbium, the medieval harbour quarter, the lately incorporated village of Pandon, three roadside extensions on the plateau with new markets and three additional churches, and six urban friaries and other religious houses in peripheral position. Before 1600 extramural suburbs had developed on all the arterial roads, followed by a downriver extension of the port during the next 100 years.

This composite plan, typical of the essentially additive changes of medieval town plans, survived almost intact to the middle of the eighteenth century when town surveys begin. From then on the old town developed as the core of an ever-growing regional capital, and the changes in its plan caused by the industrial revolution became transformative rather than additive. This left some traditional features as inherited outlines acting as a morphological frame for subsequent alterations but obliterated others.

There are three distinct kinds of changes:

(1) those representing additions to the street system;

(2) those associated with areas showing the characteristic strip-shaped plots known as burgages and representing originally the holdings of the enfranchised members of a medieval borough;

(3) those associated with the ancient town fringe along the town wall.

We shall follow these changes through successive stages in order to understand their effect on the present plan.

Corbridge's plan of 1723 (Fig. 5) shows the salient features of the medieval town. Serried lines of row houses occupied most of the street frontages with contiguous accessory buildings at their back on land divided generally in the form of rows of burgages or burgage series, the elongation of burgages varying but reaching a maximum of 6·75:1 in the north-east.

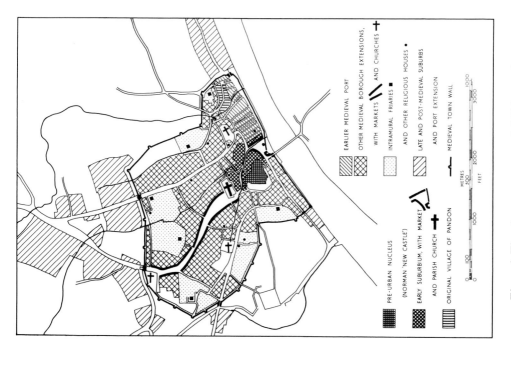

Legend (Figure 4)

PRE-URBAN NUCLEUS
(NORMAN 'NEW CASTLE')

EARLY SUBURBIUM, WITH MARKET
AND PARISH CHURCH

ORIGINAL VILLAGE OF PANDON

EARLIER MEDIEVAL PORT

OTHER MEDIEVAL BOROUGH EXTENSIONS,
WITH MARKETS AND CHURCHES

INTRAMURAL FRIARIES
AND OTHER RELIGIOUS HOUSES

LATE AND POST-MEDIEVAL SUBURBS
AND PORT EXTENSION

MEDIEVAL TOWN WALL

METRES
500   1000
FEET
1000   2000   3000

Figure 4. The plan components of old Newcastle.

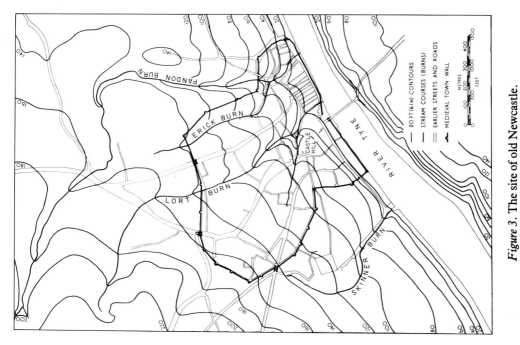

ERICK BURN

LORT BURN

PANDON BURN

CASTLE HILL

RIVER TYNE

SKINNER BURN

20 FT (6.1 m) CONTOURS

STREAM COURSES (BURNS)

EARLIER STREETS AND ROADS

MEDIEVAL TOWN WALL

METRES
100   200   300   400
FEET

Figure 3. The site of old Newcastle.

Buildings were concentrated on the burgage heads, the burgage tails being left as yards and gardens. Building coverage, i.e. the percentage of land covered by buildings, thus reflected the sizes of street-blocks and the concentration of commercial and industrial land uses at the burgage heads. Varying from one burgage to another, its averages for individual street-blocks are of some significance, though accurate measurements are impossible on Corbridge's plan. Maxima occurred generally in the busy retail centres of the town and along the commercially-used waterfront, including the south-east where merchants' offices and warehouses were arranged in tightly built-up yards and alleys or "chares" at right angles to the waterfront in a fashion common to medieval seaports.

The market place on the plateau had been occupied by tiny blocks of houses without attached burgages. Originating from temporary market stalls and vaguely conforming to the shape of the market place as its morphological frame, this late- and post-medieval market colonization is a common phenomenon.

On the Castle Hill the medieval stronghold, long since obsolete as a fortress, survived in part as a residual feature, its site being increasingly colonized by site successors such as public buildings and houses.

For centuries the town wall had formed the fixation line for the stationary urban fringe which it divided into two vaguely belt-like parts (Fig. 5). Except in the harbour area, the intramural had rather large plots containing prominent buildings, the site successors and often the functional heirs of the medieval religious houses. The largest of them was the "New House" with "The Nuns" in the north. In the extramural, arterial ribbons alternated with large open areas and occasional isolated buildings or clusters of houses, except for the river and its bridge.

On Thompson's plan of 1746 (Fig. 6) the most significant change is a tendency for the burgage tails to fill up with accessory buildings of various kinds and occasional meeting-houses, thus increasing the building coverages. This process of gradual repletion affected particularly burgages with commercially valuable street or river frontage. It reflected the increasing volume of economic activities in the regional capital during a period of general technological improvements in industry and transport.

The urban fringe showed few changes (Fig. 6). In the south-western intramural some large houses colonized the secluded site of a former friary at Hanover Square with a pleasant view over the river. In the extramural a few cottages were added to the arterial ribbons, and a variety of open spaces appeared elsewhere.

On Hutton's plan of 1770 (Fig. 7) continued burgage repletion increased building coverages generally, especially in the old centre (cf. Fig. 13). Within the urban fringe, building colonization grew in the intramural, Charlotte Square in the west being analogous to the earlier Hanover Square (Fig. 7). In the extramural new buildings were either industrial premises finding no room inside the old town, or large houses and institutions seeking the amenities of the countryside in proximity to the town.

Oliver's plan of 1830 (Fig. 8) shows the city at the end of the first phase of the industrial revolution with its quickening pace of economic and social life, after the

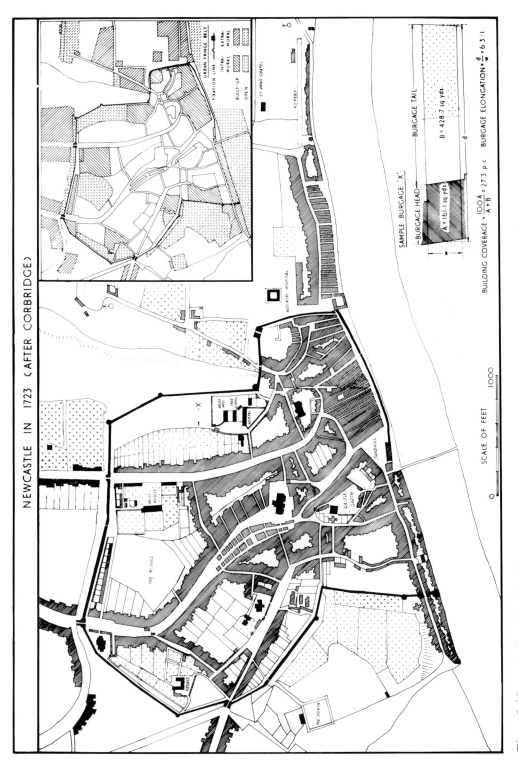

Figure 5. Newcastle in 1723 (after Corbridge).

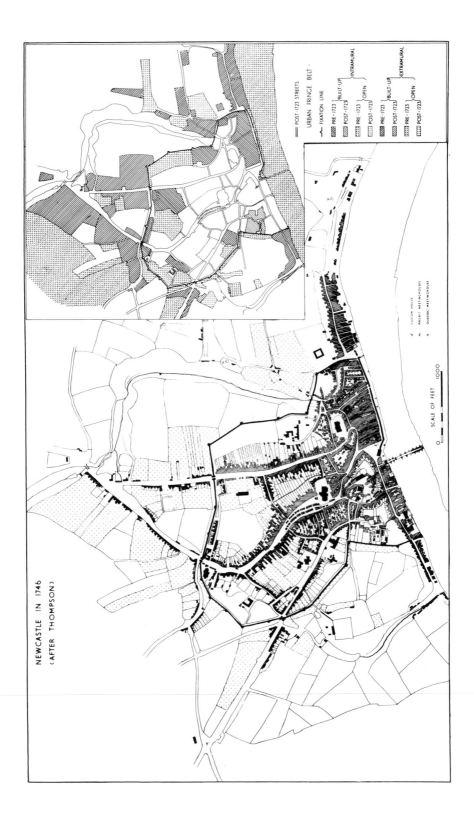

Figure 6. Newcastle in 1746 (after Thompson).

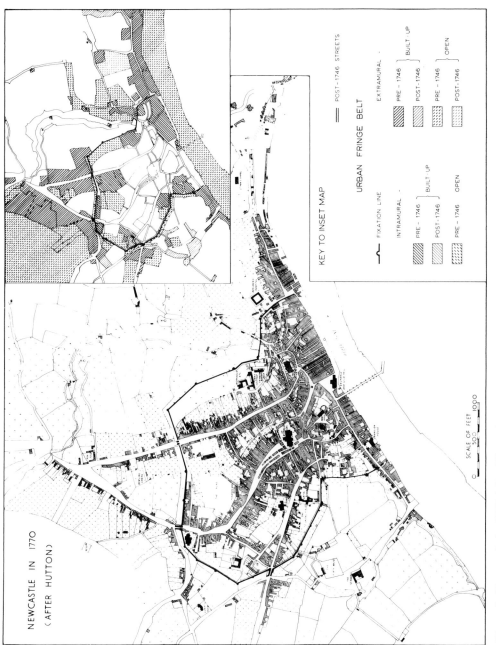

NEWCASTLE IN 1770
(AFTER HUTTON)

KEY TO INSET MAP

FIXATION LINE

INTRAMURAL -

PRE - 1746 ⎤ BUILT - UP
POST - 1746 ⎦

PRE - 1746 OPEN

URBAN FRINGE BELT

EXTRAMURAL -

PRE - 1746 ⎤ BUILT - UP
POST - 1746 ⎦

PRE - 1746 ⎤ OPEN
POST - 1746 ⎦

POST - 1746 STREETS

SCALE OF FEET

0   500   1000

Figure 7. Newcastle in 1770 (after Hutton).

URBAN FRINGE BELT-
⌐ FIXATION LINE
▦ WEAKENED AND PARTLY
   ALIENATED PORTIONS
INTRAMURAL:-
▨ PRE-1770 ⎫
▨ POST-1770 ⎬ BUILT-UP
▨ PRE-1770 OPEN
EXTRAMURAL:-
▨ PRE-1770 ⎫
▨ POST-1770 ⎬ BUILT-UP
▨ PRE-1770 ⎫
▨ POST-1770 ⎬ OPEN

═══ POST-1770 STREETS
▦ AUGMENT. REDEVEL.
EXAMPLES OF -
a DERIVATIVE PLOTS
b REPLETIVE ABSORPTION
▭ ACCRETIONS OTHER THAN URB. FRINGE BELT

METRES
0   100   200   300
0   500   1000
FEET

Figure 8. Newcastle in 1830 (Oliver's plan).

great improvements in land communications during the Regency period but before the advent of the railway. A new system of rectilinear thoroughfares, unlike the medieval streets, considerably improved internal connections across the awkward denes of the Lort Burn in the very centre of the town. A number of new streets appeared also within and beyond the urban fringe.

Increasing burgage repletion (cf. Fig. 13) showed two new forms both involving tail-end truncation. Typical late-comers in the town plan such as the new Butcher Market and a great many Nonconformist chapels colonized the burgage tails on their own derivative plots carved off from parent burgages. Elsewhere commercial and industrial premises, already occupying individual burgage tails, were spreading over adjoining burgages in a process of repletive absorption.

Outside the burgage series, new public buildings formed prominent site successors, for example the County Courts on the Castle Hill. The new streets in the centre simultaneously augmented the street system and created new street frontages with rectilinear plots, thus substituting the traditional burgage pattern by augmentative redevelopment. This represented a significant improvement of the commercial centre.

Along the old urban fringe changes were even greater. The surviving stretches of the town wall continued to attract land-use units seeking peripheral location. Thus a characteristic accumulation of late-comers, such as Nonconformist chapels, new community services, and growing industries reorganized on larger sites, together with existing open spaces, formed now a more or less continuous, rapidly expanding urban fringe belt about the wall as its ancient fixation line.[3]

In the north and north-east, however, the town wall disappeared in large stretches, giving way to a series of consequent roads under the pressure of functional changes engendered by the vigorous accretionary growth beyond. Though attracting chapels and institutions at first, their fringe-belt character was weakened in the extramural before it could assert itself fully. On the other sides of the old town new accretions were generally too small and too distant to affect the character of the intervening fringe belt.

The first Ordnance Survey plan of 1858–9 (Fig. 9) shows revolutionary changes in the old town, now the commercial heart of a major industrial region of Britain. A great central improvement scheme with new streets and compact plots provided much better internal connections and an entirely new business centre in addition to the old one. Its augmentative redevelopment, involving the filling-up of most of the Lort Burn dene, obliterated the great fringe-belt unit of the New House or Anderson Place and a good deal of the traditional burgage pattern. It pulled the gravity centre of the growing CBD northward towards the street junction at Grey's Monument. This northward development was retarded a little by the railway which tended to draw CBD expansion southward towards the new Central Station and the new London arterial road over the High Level Bridge. In the Quayside area clearance due to a fire occasioned more augmentative redevelopment of CBD character.

As a result of these profound changes the burgage pattern on the plateau shrank

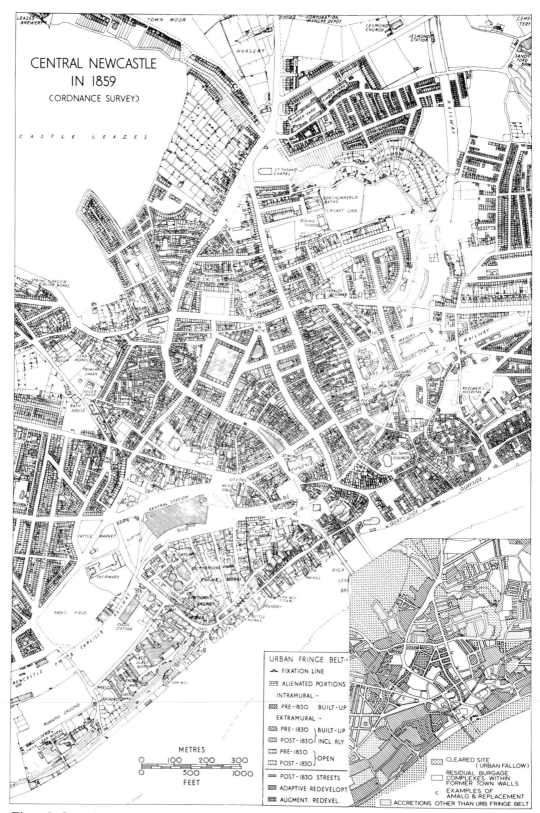

Figure 9. Central Newcastle in 1859 (after Ordnance Survey).

in area and developed into a number of disconnected burgage complexes. Repletion, having reached its climax in the central burgages, continued in the peripheral ones in response to CBD growth (cf. Fig. 13). Here and there amalgamation of contiguous burgages associated with building replacement at the burgage heads was a significant new feature. Elsewhere temporarily cleared sites were awaiting redevelopment in response to the new changes in site circumstances. On the market-place the new town hall represented adaptive redevelopment, i.e. within the framework of existing streets.

The ancient fringe belt was transformed considerably. In the north most of its intramural and the weakened proximal stretch of its extramural near the ancient fixation line was alienated, and thus ousted from its traditional position by augmentative redevelopment and accretions of a different character. This left few residual belt features among the new forms of compact CBD expansion. Instead, the growth of the belt on this side shifted spontaneously to the open distal extramural of the Castle Leazes, the Town Moor and Pandon Dene where railway construction soon affirmed the fringe-belt character.

Sandwiched between the old town and the new accretions outside, fringe-belt development began to turn from exclusive expansion to consolidation with the accumulation of new chapels, institutions, and industries or the repletive growth of old ones. In the south-west, however, the railway caused the belt to expand considerably.

The growth of the extramural showed a varying relation to the new residential accretions adjoining it. In the Blenheim Street area in the west small industrial units originated in general fringe-belt location simultaneously with contemporary, but functionally unrelated, residential accretions. The latter formed the matrix in which the former were embedded. Clearly this "porphyritic" arrangement expresses the formative influence of a fringe-belt context on adjoining accretionary growth of otherwise residential character and thus represents a fringe-belt aureole. It is typical of the early and mid-Victorian accretionary growth of smaller houses fronting streets in long terraces and leaving more or less awkward "back" sites in the interior of street blocks. In the absence of planning control of any kind, the latter were colonized by industrial fringe-belt units.

In the east near the Keelmen's Hospital the relation of fringe belt to residential accretions differed. Here conditions of landownership had kept the fringe belt open until the new accretions on its east side were well advanced. The latter, however, like the older area to the south, lacked most of the elementary institutional services, and when the open land became available for building, schools and public baths began to colonize it in a compact zone. This was part of the fringe belt genetically but owed its character to its functional connection with the adjoining residential accretions. In other words, the aureole effect here worked in the reverse direction and emanated from the residential accretions. Thus the dispersed fringe-belt aureole of the Blenheim Street area contrasts with the compact aureole near the Keelmen's Hospital in terms of functional significance and topographical arrangement.

Another fringe-belt change concerns the relation of extramural to intramural. At Central Station and at Manors Station railway installation resulted in fixation-line transgression, i.e. the encroachment of the proximal extramural on the intramural across the newly effaced fixation line.

The Ordnance Survey plans of 1894–1906 (Fig. 10) show a continuation of all these major changes in a period of greatly increased industrial and commercial traffic and of expanding social and community services. Additions to the street system extended the CBD towards the Central Station, completed the augmentative redevelopment in the port area, improved urgently needed connections across the former Pandon Dene to the vigorously developing industrial areas on the lower river, and aided fringe-belt expansion in various parts besides accompanying accretionary growth outside it.

In the residual burgage complexes changes due to CBD intensification continued. Ordinary repletion had largely reached its climax, but repletive absorption became more prominent, especially where augmentative redevelopment, reducing the burgage area still further, created new streets along individual burgage plots. Amalgamation with associated replacement at the street front increased, affecting burgage complexes as well as earlier redevelopment.

Transformation was greatest in the ancient fringe belt. In the south-west, where the Central Station cut off a section of the old town and its former fringe zone from the CBD, a massive railway, industrial and warehouse area had by now overwhelmed the once residential district round Hanover Square and was expanding south-westward. In the north-west, belt development began to assume a similar scale but a different, more institutional character. In the north-east and east, industries, institutions and the railway invaded the Pandon Dene area, the process being facilitated by large-scale levelling of the Dene, creating temporarily cleared sites or urban fallow in preparation for the new layouts.

Elsewhere fringe-belt growth proceeded more piecemeal and with a good deal of site succession, often among kindred land-use units and usually accompanied by substantial increase in building coverage in the form of large building units. Similarly, dispersed and compact aureole phenomena, already observed in the previous period, were emphasized in this one. In the older parts of the belt near the ancient fixation line, some sites reverted to the fringe belt after temporary alienation. Others yielded to CBD expansion, the alienation being small but foreshadowing more extensive redevelopment. In a few cases the intramural impinged upon burgage complexes by repletive absorption.

Thus everywhere the inner fringe belt not only kept but emphasized its own identity in spite of the vigorous accretionary growth of the city beyond it. Though its areal expansion had not ceased, consolidation had now become more important.

The Ordnance Survey plan of 1940 (Fig. 11) shows two important additions to the central street-plan: an eastward extension of Market Street, and the new Tyne Bridge which relocated the Great North Road through central Newcastle and so promoted modern CBD growth along its new, more easterly line.[4]

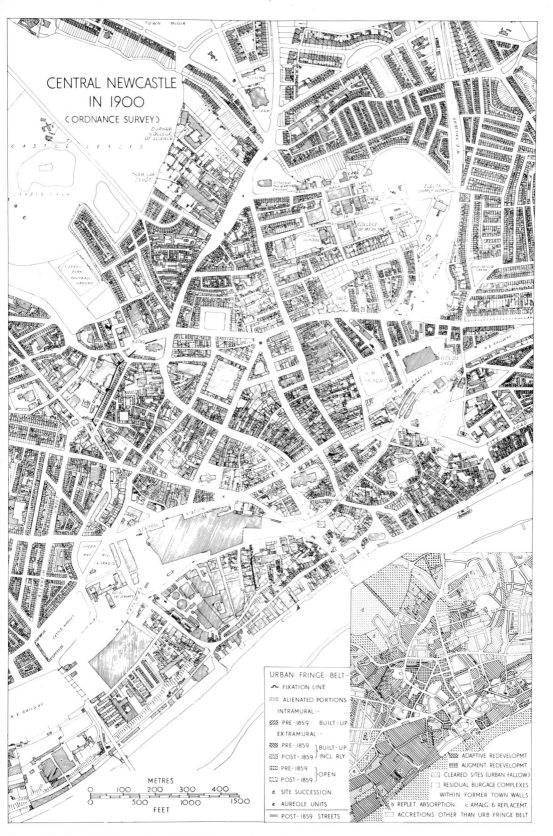

Figure 10. Central Newcastle in 1900 (after Ordnance Survey).

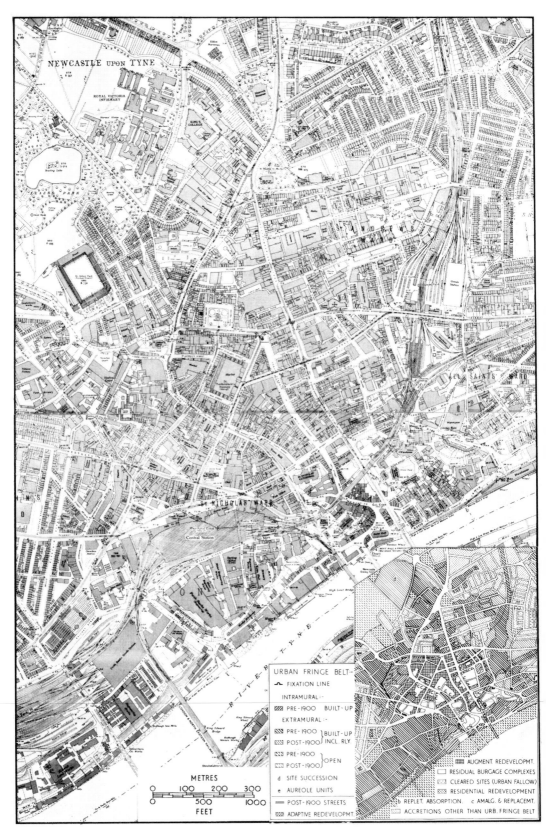

Figure 11. Central Newcastle in 1940. Reproduced from the Ordnance Survey map with the permission of the Controller of Her Majesty's Stationery Office, Crown copyright reserved.

CBD development transformed the nearly saturated residual burgage pattern considerably by further amalgamation of burgages with striking building replacements, by repletive absorption, by temporary clearance, and by central redevelopment. Ultimately all this amounted to progressive obliteration of the old pattern but affected the city differentially because of the shifts in CBD growth largely in response to changes in the major river crossings.

Two forms of CBD growth assumed general significance beyond their effect on the dwindling burgage complexes. Amalgamation and replacement was now associated with all types of central plan units and with the functional importance of the two north–south arteries, especially the Great North Road. Central redevelopment, mainly of the adaptive kind, expanded the CBD northward and became the standard type of fringe-belt alienation along the Great North Road. It also affected earlier residential accretions in this area.

In the inner fringe belt as a whole consolidation continued, particularly with the growth of the large institutions in the north-west. Along the east–west arterials of New Bridge Street and Westgate Road the fringe belt encroached on early ribbon accretions. This change from residential to commercial function left the plots and their original buildings virtually intact but resulted in striking repletion.

In the accretions just beyond the inner fringe belt a significant change introduced slum clearance in preparation for residential redevelopment, distinct from the two forms of commercial or "central" redevelopment of the CBD.

Since 1940 amalgamation and replacement in the old town and consolidation of the inner fringe belt have continued (Fig. 12).

Interpretation

Having followed the plan development of central Newcastle in some detail over a span of 230 years, we may now interpret the existing plan as its geographical result. While the development has been slow and additive during the six centuries before 1723, it has become accelerated and transformative since the beginning of the industrial revolution. Three major processes are involved in the changes of this later period—the transformation of the burgage pattern, commercial redevelopment, and fringe-belt development.

The burgage pattern has been transformed in two ways: by building repletion and by a metamorphosis of the actual plot pattern. In the old kernels of present-day cities building repletion is functionally varied according to the economic and social impulses of different periods. It can be measured in terms of building coverage. This is adequate for plan analysis, though one should remember that in cities building repletion proceeds not only horizontally but also vertically by an increase in the number of storeys or floor-space concentration. But this leads beyond the scope of plan analysis and serves as a reminder that plan, buildings and land-use pattern are all complementary aspects of urban morphology. Though repletion varies from one burgage to another, part or the whole of a burgage series commonly experiences it in a similar way. Thus its average building coverage can

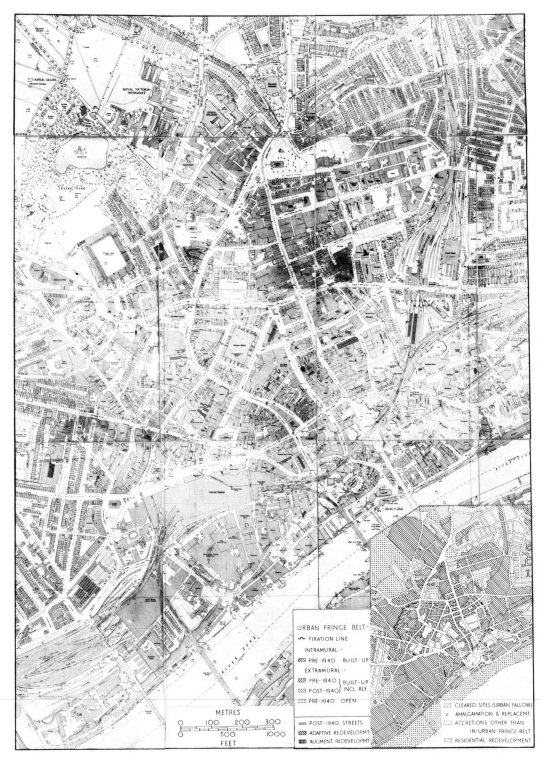

Figure 12. Central Newcastle in 1954. Reproduced from the Ordnance Survey map with the permission of the Controller of Her Majesty's Stationery Office, Crown copyright reserved.

be significant, especially in the case of residual burgage complexes of later stages as long as these do not become too small (Fig. 13).

Whether viewed in terms of individual burgages or in those of burgage series, building repletion appears as a cyclic process showing in succession institutive, repletive, climax, and recessive phases. It may be called the burgage cycle and, where completed, is terminated by the demolition of buildings and the obliteration of plots in preparation for redevelopment (Figs 13 and 14). This final stage of temporarily waste land is the specifically urban form of Hartke's *Sozialbrache* and may be termed urban fallow.[5] It can vary greatly in length of time.

Today individual burgages have reached different stages in accordance with their own circumstances and thus display the cycle most clearly. Limited evidence in respect of typical English long burgages (elongation more than 5 to 1) so far suggests the following representative ranges of building coverage for various phases of the burgage cycle: institutive phase *c*. 10–30, repletive phase *c*. 30–60 for market towns or up to *c*. 70 for regional capitals, climax phase *c*. 60–100 (*c*. 70–100 for regional capitals).

In burgage series, on the other hand, the cycle in terms of average building coverage can be obscured by the accelerated reduction in area of many series during the last 100 years. These, though showing an apparent increase in building coverage, have in fact lost a number of burgages in which the cycle has run its course or has been interrupted by other forms of development.

A random reconnaissance suggests that the burgage cycle occurs elsewhere in Europe and that this paper demonstrates a regional variant due to the generally great elongation of English burgages and the peculiarities of English economic history. It should also be noted that repletion can affect other plan units besides ancient burgage land.

Apart from repletion there is the metamorphosis of the plot pattern of burgages. This is a varied and gradual process of tail-end truncation, repletive absorption, especially in burgage tails, and above all amalgamation often associated with the replacement of dominant buildings at the burgage heads. Through progressive amalgamation it tends to result in increasing plot concentration. This can be measured as the average amount of plot area in square yards per yard of plot boundaries. Incidentally, absence of information as to what are true plot boundaries on Ordnance Survey maps introduces a possible source of error in the measurement of plot concentration. Plot metamorphosis obliterates the burgage pattern by stages, leading from the essentially intact or orthomorphic to the hypometamorphic and the metamorphic pattern. The affected burgage series are reduced to residual burgage complexes and eventually completely obliterated.

Though often associated with one another, repletion and plot metamorphosis are two distinct processes and show no constant relation in their rates of progress or their phases. While repletion is a very general phenomenon in English towns, plot metamorphosis, at any rate in its more advanced stages, requires the stronger economic impulses of the larger city and its central thoroughfares. Consequently existing burgage complexes exhibit a variety of phase combinations of the two

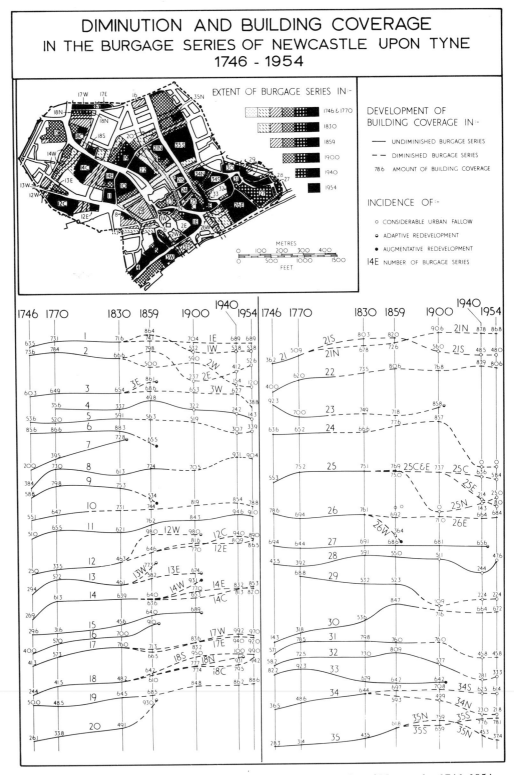

Figure 13. Diminution and building coverage in the burgage series of Newcastle, 1746–1954.

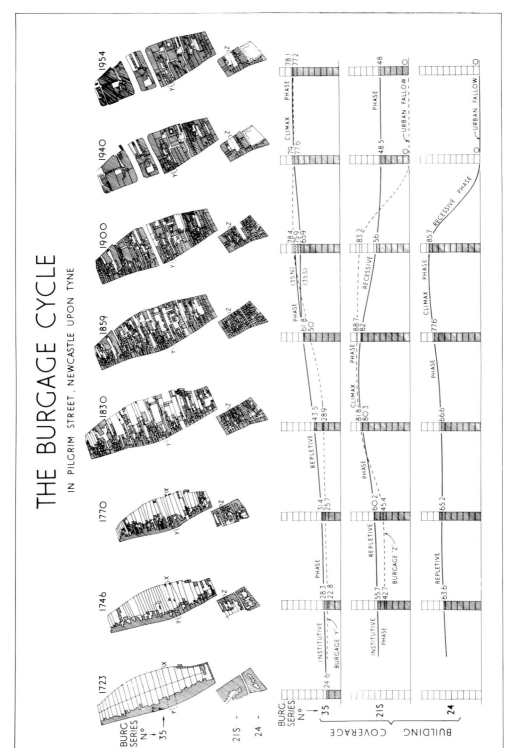

Figure 14. The burgage cycle in Pilgrim Street, Newcastle. Crown copyright reserved.

processes involved and thus a number of evolutionary types (Fig. 15). Of these the more unaltered types tend to be absent from central Newcastle as they do not generally survive the more forceful economic development of city centres but are frequently found in small market towns.[6] The Quayside of Newcastle, owing to its particular form of ancient strip plots associated with their commercial function in a fringe-belt context, adds a special variant of its own.

However the two processes are interrelated in particular localities, they must ultimately come to an end either by running their full course or by interruption in preparation for subsequent redevelopment. Except in the rarer cases of amalgamation without building replacement or very gradual transition from plot metamorphosis to piecemeal redevelopment, the final stage of complete burgage obliteration is marked by the occurrence of urban fallow.

The second major process affecting the city centre is commercial redevelopment, creating a new plot pattern without reference to the lineaments of the preceding traditional one.[7] It can be of two kinds. Redevelopment of a block of land within the framework of existing streets is adaptive, while that involving the creation of new streets is augmentative (Fig. 16).

Adaptive redevelopment comprises two types, the first involving a radical change of plot pattern and the second being effected by gradual, piecemeal redevelopment, usually associated with the metamorphic phase of plot concentration. Good examples of the latter are presented by burgage complex 15 from 1859 to 1940 and burgage complex 18 N from 1830 to 1954 (Fig. 13). In such cases the distinction between the metamorphic phase of the burgage cycle and adaptive redevelopment is inevitably somewhat artificial. It can only be based conventionally on some particular quantitative limit of plot concentration.

Redevelopment may interrupt the burgage cycle and plot metamorphosis in any one of their respective phases. Moreover, it is by no means restricted to ancient burgage land but—like repletion—can affect other plan units.

Besides commercial redevelopment in the centre of the city there is also residential redevelopment in the slum belt in and around the inner urban fringe belt. It is generally augmentative if the affected site is large.

The third major process is fringe-belt development (Fig. 17). Louis's *Stadtrandzone* in the sense of a continuous or closed fringe belt following an ancient fortification line round the inner city applies to Newcastle. This inner fringe belt represents one of two variants found in English towns. It develops essentially as a varied assortment of land-use units seeking peripheral location, mostly as latecomers in the town plan. Thus it is made up of institutions, warehouses, industries, large houses, cottages, and open spaces in a generally irregular arrangement. Once established, the fringe belt is perpetuated, expanded and consolidated in piecemeal fashion by accumulation, repletion and site succession long after it has ceased to be the actual town fringe.

Starting from its original fixation line, the belt expands into the old town with a relatively close-grained intramural of more stringent morphological frame, and outward with a larger, more coarse-grained extramural in conditions of greater

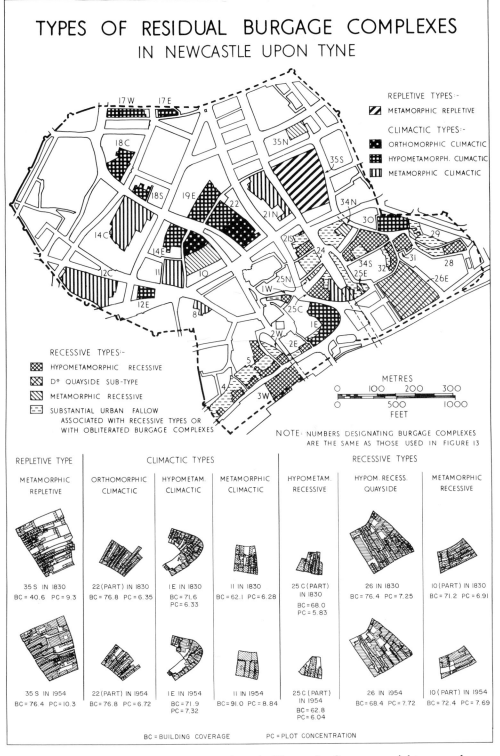

Figure 15. Types of residual burgage complexes in Newcastle. Crown copyright reserved.

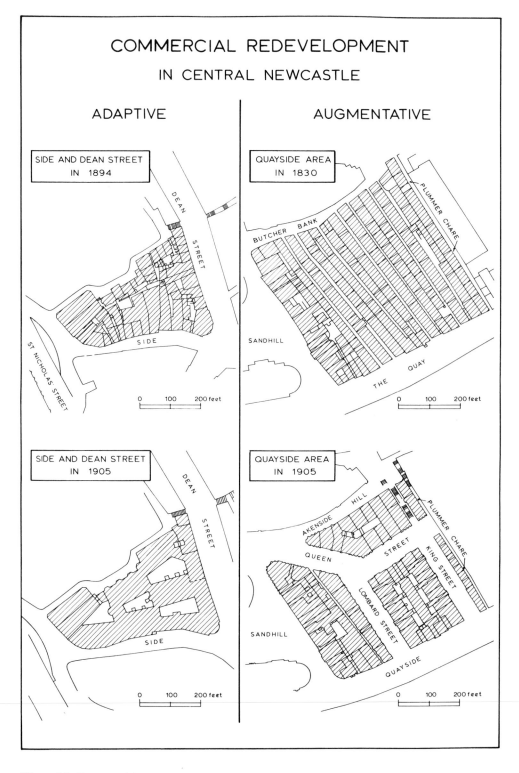

Figure 16. Commercial redevelopment in central Newcastle.

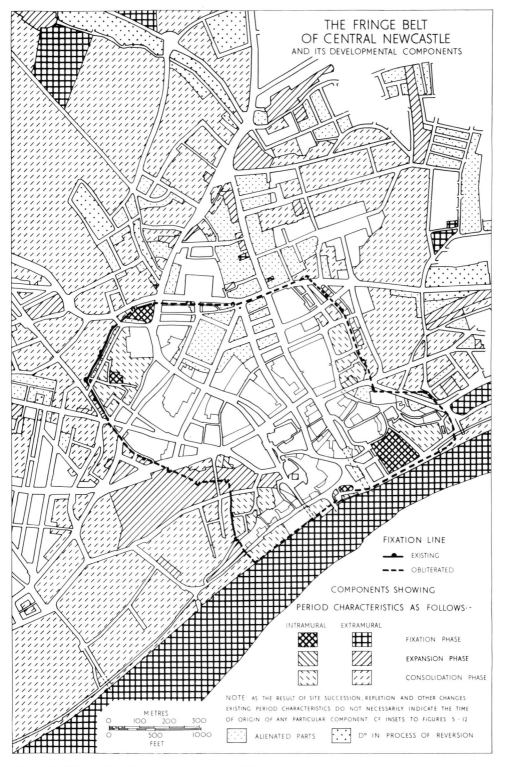

THE FRINGE BELT
OF CENTRAL NEWCASTLE
AND ITS DEVELOPMENTAL COMPONENTS

FIXATION LINE

EXISTING

OBLITERATED

COMPONENTS SHOWING

PERIOD CHARACTERISTICS AS FOLLOWS:-

INTRAMURAL   EXTRAMURAL

FIXATION PHASE

EXPANSION PHASE

CONSOLIDATION PHASE

NOTE AS THE RESULT OF SITE SUCCESSION, REPLETION AND OTHER CHANGES
EXISTING PERIOD CHARACTERISTICS DO NOT NECESSARILY INDICATE THE TIME
OF ORIGIN OF ANY PARTICULAR COMPONENT. CF INSETS TO FIGURES 5 - 12

ALIENATED PARTS   D° IN PROCESS OF REVERSION

METRES
0   100   200   300

0   500   1000
FEET

Figure 17. Fringe-belt development in central Newcastle.

morphological freedom. The vigorously growing CBD of a large city, however, generally inhibits the expansion of the intramural, while fixation-line transgression brings the extramural in closer contact with the CBD.

Three phases of fringe-belt development can be recognized. First, there is a fixation phase, when the town wall is established with its contiguous accessories such as wall streets and ditches and when arterial ribbon development is established just outside the ancient gates[8] (in Newcastle c. 1300 – c. 1700). This is followed by an expansion phase, when intramural and extramural grow (c. 1700 – c. 1860). Finally, there is a consolidation phase (post-1860), when the extramural is hemmed in by accretionary town growth outside and when functional segregation in the old town causes the belt to intensify its attraction for kindred land-use units, especially industries, warehouses and institutions, accompanied by increased site succession within its area.

Simultaneously with this development, but concentrated mainly within its consolidation phase, there is progressive functional segregation within the inner fringe belt, a spontaneous "sorting-out" of land-use units into recognizable functional sections, particularly in the extramural. Already observable in the smaller market town,[9] this phenomenon is rather more marked in the large city. In Newcastle the railway, industrial and warehouse section in the south-south-west is an earlier example and the institutional section in the north-west a more recent one. Since 1954 in fact, the consolidation and renewed growth of this part of the inner fringe belt has assumed more spectacular proportions, partly at the cost of adjoining accretions. The Royal Victoria Infirmary is expanding westward, while King's College—soon to become an independent university—is growing southward and northward by redevelopment in substitution of existing fringe-belt and accretionary property of different function. To the east of it the erection of Newcastle's new town hall, now in progress on a large and expanding site of urban fallow, inaugurates the extensive development of the future civic centre. All these latest changes represent a new phase in functional segregation and fringe-belt growth proceeding no longer spontaneously but within the more propitious framework of modern town-planning control. Within this institutional section therefore there is now predetermined segregation of a second order into distinct hospital, university and civic centre "precincts".

Functional developments affect the growth of the closed fringe belt differentially: negatively in the case of fringe-belt alienation, accompanied by a shift of growth from proximal to distal extramural; positively by sustained extramural expansion, often accelerated by the railways and the greatly increased institutional requirements of modern society.

The complex result of all the processes described is the present plan of the inner city, presenting an intricate pattern of morphogenetic types of plan units (Fig. 18). The pre-urban nucleus and the sites of the four old churches represent the earlier residual components. Among them the castle has been most affected by plot metamorphosis and site succession. The same is true of the residual burgage complexes now forming an irregular and disjointed patchwork of varied types

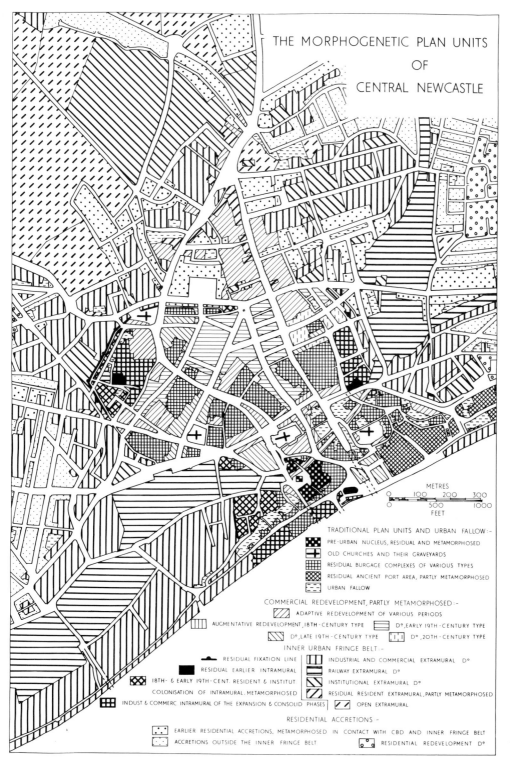

THE MORPHOGENETIC PLAN UNITS
OF
CENTRAL NEWCASTLE

METRES
0   100   200   300
0   500   1000
FEET

TRADITIONAL PLAN UNITS AND URBAN FALLOW:-
PRE-URBAN NUCLEUS, RESIDUAL AND METAMORPHOSED
OLD CHURCHES AND THEIR GRAVEYARDS
RESIDUAL BURGAGE COMPLEXES OF VARIOUS TYPES
RESIDUAL ANCIENT PORT AREA, PARTLY METAMORPHOSED
URBAN FALLOW

COMMERCIAL REDEVELOPMENT, PARTLY METAMORPHOSED:-
ADAPTIVE REDEVELOPMENT OF VARIOUS PERIODS
AUGMENTATIVE REDEVELOPMENT, 18TH-CENTURY TYPE   D°, EARLY 19TH-CENTURY TYPE
D°, LATE 19TH-CENTURY TYPE   D°, 20TH-CENTURY TYPE

INNER URBAN FRINGE BELT:-
RESIDUAL FIXATION LINE   INDUSTRIAL AND COMMERCIAL EXTRAMURAL D°
RESIDUAL EARLIER INTRAMURAL   RAILWAY EXTRAMURAL D°
18TH- & EARLY 19TH-CENT. RESIDENT & INSTITUT   INSTITUTIONAL EXTRAMURAL D°
COLONISATION OF INTRAMURAL, METAMORPHOSED   RESIDUAL RESIDENT EXTRAMURAL, PARTLY METAMORPHOSED
INDUST & COMMERC INTRAMURAL OF THE EXPANSION & CONSOLID PHASES   OPEN EXTRAMURAL

RESIDENTIAL ACCRETIONS -
EARLIER RESIDENTIAL ACCRETIONS, METAMORPHOSED IN CONTACT WITH CBD AND INNER FRINGE BELT
ACCRETIONS OUTSIDE THE INNER FRINGE BELT   RESIDENTIAL REDEVELOPMENT D°

Figure 18. The morphogenetic plan units of central Newcastle.

within the walled town. This is due partly to redevelopment and partly to the ravages of the burgage cycle which has left much urban fallow in the lower town, especially on steeply sloping sites offering greater resistance to redevelopment. The contrast between the relatively stagnating riverside town and the economically more vigorous plateau town with its three arterials is a recurrent theme in the plan of the old town and is well reflected in the types of burgage complexes (Fig. 15). Recessive types and their associated urban fallow predominate in the lower town, rarely reaching an advanced stage of plot metamorphosis, while climactic and repletive types hold the field on the plateau. Most of these show already a metamorphic plot pattern, especially along the new Great North Road. Suggestive also is the contrast between complexes 22 and 35 S (Fig. 13). The former, truncated in the past, has reached the climax of repletion on its reduced site but, lying now in a backwater of the central traffic system, has been little affected by plot metamorphosis, let alone redevelopment. The latter, because of its unusual burgage depth, is still in its repletive stage but, situated on the Great North Road, has been subject to considerable plot metamorphosis, with some striking building replacements.

Commercial redevelopment presents augmentative plan types from almost every phase of the industrial revolution. Rectilinearity in plot shapes rather than street alignment distinguishes these plan types from the burgage patterns, but the finer period variations among them are now often obscured by subsequent plot metamorphosis. From the beginning the augmentative types were associated with CBD development which explains their central position and their predominance in the plateau town. Adaptive redevelopment has the same functional background but, being more suited to small-scale or piecemeal application, has generally occurred in a more peripheral distribution. Its preponderance in the north is characteristically connected with the spontaneous CBD expansion of this part.

The inner fringe belt surrounds the business city completely, though its ancient fixation line has long ceased to be continuous and the CBD has expanded northward across it. This has been possible by partial alienation and associated shift of emphasis to the distal zone of the belt. During such change the affected fixation line as well as the intramural and proximal extramural vanished except for isolated residual features. The relocated belt appears thus entirely as a continuation of the undisturbed extramural to the south.

The intramural, now greatly reduced in size by the encroachment of central redevelopment in response to CBD pressure on available space and by fixation-line transgression, retains few plan types. Residual plan features are generally historic buildings, usually the site successors of early religious houses. Earlier residential colonization of their commonly large plots survives only in more or less metamorphosed form. Along the river and in the eastern intramural industrial and commercial development has expanded, in the former case on ancient burgage land by fringe-belt expansion in such a gradual way as hardly to constitute redevelopment, in the latter case by site succession and colonization of an earlier open space.

The much larger extramural is highly irregular in outline, street system, plot sizes and functional components, the latter constituting the actual plan types and segregating themselves increasingly in distinct functional sections.

A peculiar phenomenon is presented by earlier residential accretions that have been affected by fringe-belt relocation and expansion. As a result of these changes virtually all of them have been absorbed functionally either by the fringe belt or by the expanding CBD. Though this absorption is not yet recognizable in the plan to any great extent, it has already changed the elevational aspect of many buildings by the appearance of additional top storeys and sooner or later is bound to manifest itself in increased plot metamorphosis.

In conclusion it may be said that evolutionary plan analysis helps to recognize the geographical structure of urban built-up areas in terms of concepts covering recurrent morphological phenomena. Its pursuit requires an appreciation of underlying economic and social processes. It specializes in the town plan but links up with work on urban building fabric and land use, thus forming an integral part of the complete analysis of the townscape. Most of the phenomena described in this paper apply to all old-established towns in Britain. It would be interesting to test the method elsewhere in the world.

Notes

1. Conzen, M. R. G. (1960) *Alnwick, Northumberland: a study in town-plan analysis* Inst. Br. Geogr. Publ. No. 27.

2. The historical background to the city's development is presented in Middlebrook, S. (1950) *Newcastle upon Tyne: its growth and achievement* (Newcastle upon Tyne).

3. For the original concept of the *Stadtrandzone* or urban fringe belt see Louis, H. (1936) "Die geographische Gliederung von Gross-Berlin", *Länderkundliche Forschung* Krebs-Festschrift, 146–71.

4. House, J. W. and Fullerton, B. (1955) "City street: a half-century of change in Northumberland Street–Pilgrim Street, Newcastle upon Tyne, 1891–1955", *Plann. Outlook* 3, 40–62.

5. Hartke, W. (1953) "Die soziale Differenzierung der Agrarlandschaft im Rhein-Main-Gebiet", *Erdkunde* 7, 11–27; Hartke, W. (1956) "Die Sozialbrache als Phänomen der geographischen Differenzierung der Landschaft", *Erdkunde* 10, 257–69.

6. Due to peculiar circumstances Alnwick does not show them either, its old town presenting hypometamorphic and metamorphic types of the repletive and recessive kinds instead. Cf. Conzen, op. cit. p. 93, Fig. 18 (note 1).

7. This specific use of the term "redevelopment" should be noted as compared with the more confusing use by many planners and architects who would include building *replacement* on an existing plot otherwise left intact.

8. That early arterial ribbons form recurrent features of inner fringe belts was imperfectly understood in the plan analysis of Alnwick, where they are treated as separate plan types and divisions. See Conzen, op. cit., Figs 20 and 21 (note 1).

9. Conzen, op. cit., pp. 58, 80–1, 106, 110, 114–15 (note 1).

THREE

Historical townscapes in Britain: a problem in applied geography*

M. R. G. CONZEN

Britain is one of the most urbanized countries in the world, some 80 per cent of its population living in urban settlements according to a conservative definition of that term. Urban areas are thus important as the daily environment of the overwhelming majority of Britain's population, as a subject of geographical investigation, and as areas in which the results of geographical work can be applied to a wide field of pressing planning problems.

Among these last the proper management of our townscapes is of special importance because of its direct effect on the quality of our environment and its long-term benefit to society, even though this benefit is not of a merely economic but an essentially social and cultural nature and as such is difficult to express, and certainly not adequately assessable, in monetary terms. With regard to our historical townscapes in particular, awareness of this difference has been slow to grow in a society that has been accustomed for more than a hundred years to put economic considerations before social ones and that finds it difficult in the present cultural crisis to keep its sense of continuity and its capacity to see things interconnected, and thus shows uncertainty in its grasp of long-term values. Therefore town planning in Britain has generally been under pressure to regard care of the historical character of a townscape as of low priority among all other claims on planning and has not been helped much in the past by ineptitude in matters of "preservation". It is well to remember, however, that the problem of how to live a rational modern life within a carefully managed cultural landscape of historical value is nothing peculiar to this country but faces many advanced societies.

There is thus a need to re-establish the case for the long-term importance of historical townscapes to modern society in this country. This does involve general consideration of the nature of the cultural landscape, of which the historical

* First published in House, J. W. (ed.) (1966) *Northern Geographical essays in honour of G. H. J. Daysh* (Newcastle upon Tyne) pp. 56–78.

townscape is a particular variant, and its relation to the society that lives in it.

In Britain as a whole the urban scene has been powerfully affected by the main phase of the industrial revolution in the nineteenth century and further urban growth in the twentieth. Yet in the majority of cases the kernels of our towns show in fact a historical townscape in the sense that existing town plan and building fabric are dominated more or less by traditional forms ranging from the medieval or even Roman era to the late-Georgian or Regency period. Because of their age and their generally central location these townscapes are particularly vulnerable under the pressure of central traffic and piecemeal or comprehensive redevelopment and pose some of the most difficult problems of urban planning. Here morphological analysis on the part of the geographer would appear to be one of the prerequisites for any informed action.

This paper is a preliminary attempt to explore the field, firstly by discussing the cultural landscape and arguing the long-term social importance of historical townscapes, secondly by considering the nature of historical townscapes in general, and thirdly by examining the old kernels of a few small historical towns selected from different parts of the country with a view to illustrating simple concepts relevant to the morphology and management of historical townscapes.

Historical townscapes and society

In earlier stages of human development a cultural landscape results from the partial transformation of the natural landscape by socially organized man. Even at higher levels of civilization nature forms an ever present substratum supporting and more or less pervading the whole landscape by contributing its own complement of forms such as landforms or plants. But at these later stages most landscapes represent the transformation of previously existing cultural landscapes.

In all cases the creation of man-made forms stems from functional impulses originating in the momentary or long-term requirements of society. In their origin, therefore, these forms are purpose-orientated. Yet in cultural landscapes with a longer period of development function and form rarely show perfect congruity because of their differential changes in time. Like the society that produces them functional requirements are dynamic and subject to a more or less accelerated rate of change depending on the level of civilization. However, the material forms created by them on the earth's surface are more or less resistant to change. Representing the translation of human aspirations into geographically located matter through the investment of human effort and capital, they share the inertia of matter and become static, the more so as no society can afford to discard all its existing landscape equipment as soon as it becomes obsolescent.

This makes accumulation of forms through time one of the fundamental morphological attributes of the landscape and in that general sense renders all cultural landscapes historical. In areas with a long sequence of sustained human effort and associated period changes in the style of civilization accumulation produces distinct historical stratification in the landscape. Where this is combined with a high distribution density of man-made forms as in our historical townscapes it can be particularly marked and is as precious as a visual amenity in the daily experience of our environment as it is important to the healthy self-identification of an urban community and to its sense of continuity of existence on the ground.

Besides accumulation there is the transformation of already existing forms which represents functional adaptation to changing needs. A wide range in the possible degree of transformation makes this form of change an intermediary between unaltered accumulation and replacement.

Where adaptation can no longer be effected satisfactorily and the associated function is at the same time stenotopic or limited to a relatively narrowly defined locality for its optimum discharge, the pressure of functional requirements is liable to result in the destruction of obsolete forms and their replacement by new ones. This affects the building fabric of CBDs in towns widely and is a powerful agent in the obliteration of historical townscapes just where their character is most marked and calls for the most skilful landscape management. Coupled with this there are often extensive changes in the street system which are even more disruptive and can alter a medieval town kernel out of all recognition.

That the progressive effacement of historical townscapes represents an irreparable cultural loss to the community has been directly or indirectly acknowledged by modern society in the repeated attempts to imitate a destroyed historical townscape in the subsequent redevelopment of its site. The Rows of Chester provide one of the better known earlier examples and the aftermath of World War II has given rise to many more in continental Europe. Positive awareness of the claims of historical townscapes in relation to modern central traffic is well exemplified by the Buchanan Report on *Traffic in towns*.[1]

Accumulation, transformation and replacement represent the dynamic changes in a cultural landscape. They are effected by society or more particularly by those groupings within it that represent at once functionally and geographically distinct variation in the mode of life of any particular civilization. These units of society are functional groups diversified in themselves and arranged on the earth's surface in adaptation to geographical conditions. As such they form the essential link between nature and civilization and are the agent of the transformation of the landscape. Urban communities represent such socio-geographical groups.[2]

As form after form is added to the earth's surface by a socio-geographical group within its area of occupancy or habitat, only some of these forms replacing earlier ones, the whole cultural landscape becomes an "objectivation of the spirit"[3] of society in its own culture context and in the historical context of its area. In Britain and all over Europe historical townscapes illustrate this theme in its regional variation. Thus in the course of time the landscape, whether that of a large region like a country or of a small locality like a market town, acquires its specific *genius loci*, its culture- and history-conditioned character which commonly reflects not only the work and the aspirations of the society at present in occupancy but also that of its precursors in the area. These attributes of the cultural landscape represent an important and unique aspect of our environment.

As the gradual accumulation of inherited and contemporary forms proceeds, congruity between current requirements and the existing landscape equipment is rendered less and less likely. This is but the manifestation on a higher level of that perennial functional conflict between social man and his habitat that has been a condition of his life on earth from the beginning. In that sense, then, the cultural landscape acquires a certain separateness of existence *vis-à-vis* its occupant society, and far from merely reflecting current requirements it refers also to, and is a cumulative if incomplete historical record of, the whole succession of human needs and aspirations as these have developed in a particular habitat. Thus it imparts the depth of time perspective and the sense of group-supported continuity to the daily awareness of our own social existence on the ground, and this is one of the prerequisites for any properly balanced relation between individual and society and between the socio-geographical group such as an urban community and its home.

In our preoccupation with current practical problems we are apt to overlook that a physical environment of the fullest possible historical expressiveness or historicity is an important asset to any healthy and expanding form of social life at advanced levels of civilization. It gives a sense of continuity and at the same time of diversity of human effort and achievement in different periods, a "tradition" not in any narrow but a wider sense and all the more effective for presenting itself visibly in man's artefacts on the earth's surface. It enables the individual and the social mind to take root in an area and in demonstrating the historical dimension of human experience stimulates comparison and through it a more informed way of reasoning. Through their historicity cultural landscapes exert an educative and regenerative influence on the mind, and this answers a fundamental long-term social requirement no less essential for being incapable of direct definition in terms of economic benefits. The importance of proper rapport between society and the *genius loci* becomes evident when in the course of a major socio-economic revolution a whole society in a sense turns its back temporarily and partially on its own historical context as happened in Britain during the Victorian phase of the industrial revolution and under the mesmerizing impact of technical innovations. The material and spiritual cost of the ensuing social and cultural crisis as that of its landscape residue can be very great and is liable to be passed on in large part to future generations. Today the partial disorientation of our education system, the tyranny of the motor car and of television and their effect on society and culture in this country indicate just another such crisis. In terms of town planning there is as yet nothing in the current treatment of historical townscapes like those of Canterbury, Norwich and many other English cities to show that as a responsible society we are at all adequately equipped to deal with the emergency.

If the historical aspect of the cultural landscape has such great long-term significance to society, historical townscapes are particularly important in an urbanized country such as Britain. With most of the rest of Europe this country shares a long and varied tradition of urban life. Though the townscapes of some of our biggest cities present few elements taking us back beyond the Georgian or even the Victorian period the vast majority of towns of all sizes present a wide range of historical forms. This reaches generally from the Middle Ages to modern times and is illustrated best in the kernels of "old towns" where we find the historical townscape *par excellence*. Because of their generally central position and their collective importance these historical townscapes present a major planning problem of considerable urgency.

In modern society the variety of functional claims on the use of land, even that of the most basic ones, is great and many of them tend to conflict. Optimum success in spatial planning means an overall maximum fulfilment of these claims not as separate elements but as a complex. This implies achievement of a particular balance between them according to the area to be planned and its society, a balance in which these claims can co-exist in progressive satisfaction. The nature of this task is not under discussion here. It does need to be emphasized, however, that the continued existence of the historical character of townscapes is a universal long-term social requirement of great importance that should have its proper place in the balance of claims on planning quite apart from the incidental economic "tourist" value attaching to any particular townscape. The critical point here is that historicity quickly becomes a wasting asset, the wastage accelerating in something like geometrical progression compared with the actual amount of destruction of traditional forms and depending also on how ill-considered the associated redevelopment is.

All this suggests "preservation" as the key note and indeed physical preservation, albeit in a complex and relative sense, is involved. But the term "preservation" has already a history in British planning discussions and in the course of it has acquired unfortunate overtones of oversimplification, excessive isolation of purpose, ineptness of method, and even crankiness on the part of those who advocate it. Preservation has suffered from lack of funds, rigidity of application and exclusiveness of concentration on buildings to the neglect of town-plan features such as street spaces and their building lines and, worst of all, preoccupation with isolated buildings of special merit as if an historical townscape were merely a loose assemblage of remarkable bits and pieces without spatial coherence or context. The geographical nature of historical townscapes as well as their role within the totality of planning claims on the land requires a more holistic approach. Instead of speaking merely of "preservation" it might be better to use the term landscape management as being less suggestive of restriction to physical preservation of particular and in a sense isolated landscape elements. To avoid misunderstanding "landscape" is used here in the comprehensive sense of the geographer, which should also be that of the planner. In the case of historical townscapes, then, preservation is a significant aspect of townscape management and some of its technical aspects will emerge from the consideration of actual townscapes later.

In the specific educational and cultural conditions of Britain today it might seem Utopian to ever expect the considerable heritage of our historical townscapes to be kept substantially. Its position is indeed precarious and it is being continuously diminished notwithstanding the nation's official commitment to "comprehensive" planning. The fact is that in a democratic society the state of the cultural landscape and in particular the preservation or neglect of its historicity reflects closely the average cultural consciousness of that society and thus indirectly the long-term efficiency of its education system. In recent years some ineptitude, even indifference, towards this heritage has not been unknown among bit cities with a great historic past and large and reputedly enlightened planning offices. Yet cities like Amsterdam or Bern, to name but two European examples that have central traffic and land-use problems as pressing as any, succeed in carrying their justly famed historical townscapes much less impaired through the present phases of their continuously expanding economic and social life. Here seems to be one subject in which planning theory needs a broader background of comparative study.

The nature of the historical townscape

Townscapes present three systematic aspects to morphological analysis expressed by the distinct form categories of town plan, building fabric, and land utilization. They are integral parts of the townscape linked together in space by a hierarchical principle. Under it the town plan "contains", and forms the morphological frame of, land and building utilization which consists of land-use units forming separate land parcels or plots. These in turn determine the building fabric contained within them.

Beyond these static links the more important ones of dynamic morphology depend on the differential time response of the three form categories to changing functional needs. Town plan and to a lesser extent building fabric are more conservative in this respect as they tend to reflect the pattern of past land ownership and capital investment. Therefore they present a greater range and quantity of traditional (pre-1850) forms and thus contribute substantially to the historicity of the townscape. Land utilization responds more easily to changing functional impulses and its influence on a historical townscape is therefore more negative. It often involves considerable replacement of traditional buildings in the CBD by modern ones and new vehicular access to the centre.

Turning now to the town plan, this is not the place to reiterate the method of town-plan analysis[4] or to apply it in detail to our five examples. However, it is relevant to remember that the town plan is not merely a "street plan" but consists of four element complexes—site, street system, plot pattern, and building arrangement. Physically they are interrelated by a hierarchical principle analogous to that governing the form categories of the whole townscape, the spatially more comprehensive complexes acting as morphological frames for the less comprehensive ones.

These element complexes combine to form plan units with marked period traits even though in the course of time individual elements are liable to change in detail.

Thus the characteristic plot pattern of serially arranged medieval strip plots or burgages survives recognizably, if modified, in virtually all our five examples.

Besides very simple plans like those of Whithorn and Frodsham (Fig. 1) there are composite medieval town plans made up of a larger number of plan units. In the case of Alnwick and Ludlow (Figs 2 and 4) this is owing to growth by stages, but in Conway (Fig. 3) compositeness occurred within a single act of foundation in articulated response to a complex but well-defined planning problem. If the simpler plans establish a more easily recognizable type and impart great strength to an otherwise small historical townscape by providing a single central focus such as a street-market space, more complex plans greatly increase the degree of uniqueness and variety of visual interest. Clearly these considerations apply to the plans of many county towns, cathedral cities and great historic ports.

Medieval plans rarely show a strictly geometrical arrangement of elements. In the case of unitary plans, as in Whithorn or Frodsham, adaptation to site conditions already tends to informalize the focal street space so that the building rows lining it are seen in curvature, quite apart from the medieval and post-medieval irregularities of building-line detail. Vistas along such street spaces tend therefore to be closed by building groups in lateral position or are at least strongly affected by them. There are of course straight medieval streets but where they occur they are usually short enough to have their vistas effectively closed by some building or other structure, not always deliberately so. In any case, the buildings lining such streets are not normally uniform because of the burgage pattern which makes for quick succession of independently designed buildings as the eye follows them. This plan arrangement is characteristic of medieval corporate society where everybody belonged to a particular group and accepted the measure of that group yet within this, certainly in towns, was recognized as an individual.

A composite medieval plan greatly increases the asymmetry in historical townscapes. Prominent buildings like castles or churches often have eccentric location. The siting of town walls is generally relief-conditioned and therefore irregular though never haphazard. Medieval markets as centres of a town's business life are differentiated as plan units from ecclesiastical, residential and other quarters.

A medieval town plan, therefore, causes the growth of the urban community in a distant historical period, its social, economic and cultural differentiation, its community aspirations and its attitude towards nature in terms of the site, to be reflected in the historical townscape by imparting to it the characteristics of irregularity, asymmetry, emphasis of particular points and frequent visual surprise. Thus the interest in historical townscapes is simultaneously historical and aesthetic.

The other great contributor to the historicity of townscapes is the traditional building fabric. Once again, systematic analysis is not appropriate in this paper[5] nor can the building types mapped in our examples be explained in detail. But a few general points about the distribution pattern of traditional building types need to be made to appreciate its effect on the character of historical townscapes.

The building fabric of towns can be readily divided according to siting and original function into those buildings that house the dominant part of the land use occupying their plots and those that serve subsidiary functions. The first are the "plot dominants" and the last the "plot accessories". In townscapes with a medieval plan, the majority of plot dominants are traditionally sited at the street frontage of their burgage plots. There they form usually serried rows of buildings and thus contribute prominently to the character of the townscape whereas most of the plot accessories do not.[6]

Within this grouping, however, each building type forms its own stock having its particular distribution pattern. This can be called the stand of the building type in question in analogy to the stand of timber in forestry or the crop stand of the American farmer. The stands of different building types associate in varying ways within the same town to form that town's unique building pattern. Any particular building group or association of groups within that pattern may consist of one building type only and therefore form an exclusive group, or it may be a mixed group characterized either by a more or less equal mixture of several building types or by the dominance of one type with an admixture of other types.

Whatever the building pattern, it is the geographical result of changes caused by functional processes in the town's history and represents a distinct aspect of dynamic morphology. In their building pattern historical townscapes reflect the age and the economic and social history of the urban community, since every period of prosperity carries its own impulse of building replacement into the townscape. Thus we must expect wide variations in the composition of these patterns, their totality over the whole country representing a national heritage as impressive in its diversity and depth of historical perspective as it is stimulating in its unending variation on the theme of the *genius loci*.

Very active periods of building replacement in English town centres have been the thirteenth century, the Elizabethan period (1560–1600), the Georgian period (1700–1850), the mid- and late-Victorian period, and the twentieth century. Of the first three, the Georgian and less so the Elizabethan periods have had the greatest influence on existing historical townscapes through the large stands of dwelling-houses they have contributed. As replacements these conformed substantially to the pre-existing medieval town plan without altering its plot pattern very much or exceeding the elevation scale of its street spaces. As a result such periods allow the Middle Ages a strong voice in the historical townscape even though few medieval building types may survive. But the medieval period finds expression not only in its town plans but in great buildings of special social importance. These are the cathedrals, parish churches, castles, and town walls with their gates. Contrary to the burgesses' dwelling-houses they dominate the urban scene by their prominent siting, their great elevation and their significance in the town silhouette. They are townscape dominants reflecting the differentiation and corporate nature of medieval society.

The harmony between the ancient street system and plot pattern and its later traditional building fabric has depended very much on the relative stability of pre-industrial society in its technology, its building methods, and in its economic, social and cultural conventions which, while allowing individual expression, kept individual effort well within the generally accepted form language of its period. The message conveyed to the observer by the resulting townscape is that of continuity of successful human aspirations in the context of a closely-knit community firmly rooted in its inherited habitat. Any row of traditional building types lining an ancient market place in Britain will illustrate the point.

In the Victorian period industrial society, in spite of promising but isolated beginnings, failed on the whole to develop an architectural form language appropriate to its new technology and production methods, its volume of capital investment and its enormous economic, demographic and civilizational expansion. Instead, the distracting influence of the new economic development on architecture caused the age to borrow its idiom from a medley of historical styles frequently without recourse to fundamental principles of composition. The effect on existing historical townscapes in Britain has been devastating. Larger towns have generally suffered more than smaller ones, but there are few market towns that do not show some Victorian indiscretion in their historic centres. Not only public buildings such as town halls and market halls have been involved in this but also quite a range of commercial buildings, notably shopfront buildings and banks.

More recently, the development of chain store organization has begun to impair even more seriously the historically grown individuality of British towns as expressed in their physiognomy, and in the present uncertainties about a really informed planning opinion in these matters the current pressure in favour of comprehensive central redevelopment can easily lead in the same direction. The ultimate result of these nation-wide tendencies could be a single brand of superurbia in which historic towns as we know them would lose their distinctive physiognomy and could become indistinguishable parts of a material environment in which society might well lose its essential sense of the continuity and diversity of human experience in time and perhaps of its whole social creativity.

To sum up, the quality of the historical townscape presented by the old kernels of British market towns rests very generally on the considerable survival of their medieval town plans and their remaining stock of traditional buildings among which townscape dominants have special importance. Land utilization, though generally keeping the kernels as business centres and in that sense as going concerns, can be more uncertain in its relation to a historical townscape because of the danger of building replacements that are architecturally unsympathetic to the traditional scale and form rhythm of the townscape and because of inadequately considered improvements of vehicular access to the centres.

Some historical townscapes in Britain

It remains to apply the results of our discussion to a few examples in order to reach some general conclusions about historical townscapes and their planning problem.

The old kernels of five small market towns in different parts of Britain have been selected. All of them present medieval town plans but vary somewhat in their building fabric. They are those of Whithorn in Galloway (1961 population 990), Frodsham in Cheshire (1951 population 5245), Alnwick in Northumberland (1961 population 7489), Conway in North Wales (1961 population 11 392) and Ludlow in Shropshire (1961 population 6774) (Figs 1–4).[7]

Whithorn's historical townscape has a very simple plan structure consisting of a small but originally important pre-urban nucleus and a fine medieval street market on its east side. The former comprises the ruins of St Ninian's priory and the Georgian parish church; the latter developed as a result of the great pilgrimage traffic and is now the main constituent of the townscape. Its central street space is individualized by a double curvature and clearly defined by serried rows of unpretentious late-Georgian (Regency) houses of two storeys and in stone, a legacy of the prosperity during the agricultural revolution, and transverse buildings at either end pointing to the position of former town gates. The whole unit, still punctuated laterally by the tower of its Georgian town hall, is typical of the traditional Scottish burgh of barony.[8]

The irruption of Victorian commercial buildings with indiscreet elevations in the northern half of the street market into which the little CBD has contracted in response to the pull of a former railway station and the main road to Newton Stewart, has been slight. Thus the modern life of this rural service centre in the bottom rank of the central-place hierarchy has left its historic townscape almost unimpaired and renders it important beyond the functional significance of the place. Townscape management, concentrating on the preservation of the street space, its street lines and building elevations, and on architectural control in the replacement of non-traditional buildings, would have little difficulty in guaranteeing its survival provided this was accepted as a firm regional rather than a merely local commitment.

Frodsham[9] has the same type of medieval street market but has lost its pre-urban nucleus and most of its traditional building types. Because of their later plaster cover the few pre-Georgian timber-frame houses otherwise characteristic of Cheshire no longer add their distinctive note to the townscape. But their distribution over the whole length of the fine street market in conjunction with the characteristic "display" curvatures of its street lines suggests investigation of the feasibility of reconstituting the unplastered timber-frame elevations and might

Figure 1. Whithorn and Frodsham.
Building types and urban land utilization: A—Ruins of St Ninian's Priory; B—Parish church; C—Georgian town hall; D—Main road to Newton Stewart; E—Main road to Chester; F—Frodsham station; G—Main road to Warrington; For key to shades see Fig. 4. *Plan units*: 1—Pre-urban nucleus; 2—Medieval suburbium (street-market layout); 3—Post-medieval fringe belt and residential accretions (traditional components); 4—Post-medieval fringe belt and residential accretions (later components). *Wall materials*: 1—Stone; 2—Timber frame, mostly plastered; 3—Brick, rarely plastered or rough-cast; 4—Vertical boarding; 5—Corrugated iron sheeting.

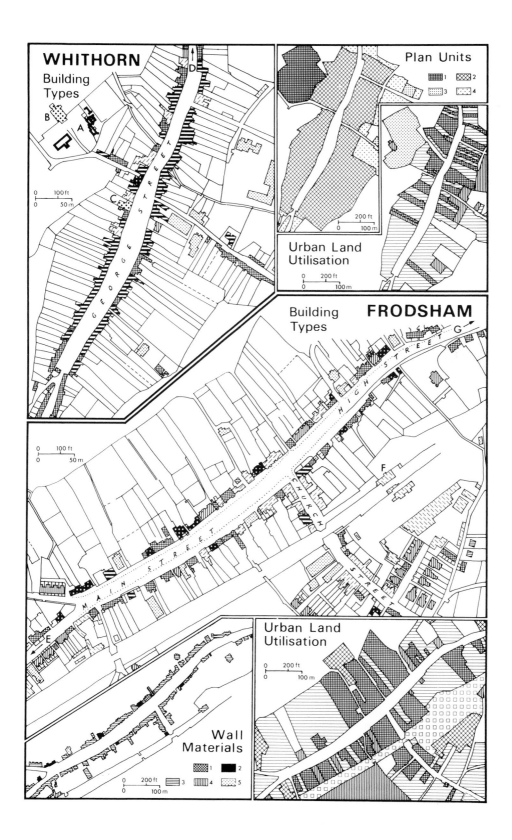

WHITHORN
Building Types

GEORGE STREET

0 100 ft
0 50 m

Plan Units
1 2
3 4

Urban Land
Utilisation

0 200 ft
0 100 m

0 200 ft
0 100 m

Building
Types   **FRODSHAM**

HIGH STREET

CHURCH STREET

MAIN STREET

0 100 ft
0 50 m

Wall
Materials
1 2
3 4 5

0 200 ft
0 100 m

Urban Land
Utilisation

0 200 ft
0 100 m

call for a combination of local cooperative effort and tangible support by the planning authority. For the rest, early-Victorian and later building replacement has been extensive in this main-road settlement and local service centre for a continuously growing residential area between several industrial districts in Lancashire and Cheshire. This modern development is also reflected in the relatively compact stand of shopfront buildings and other commercial structures within Frodsham's little CBD around the Church Street junction and railway station.

Frodsham's historical townscape, then, is weaker than that of Whithorn because of its very mixed building stock in which traditional types no longer dominate. Yet the great central street market emphasizes considerably the historical element in Frodsham's character. Proper townscape management should include preservation of the existing central street space with its trees and cobbled sides, preservation and as far as possible elevational restitution of traditional building types, and elevational control of new development in terms of scale, form rhythm and building materials.

Alnwick shows similarity to Whithorn in the clear dominance of its Georgian building types but differs from Whithorn and Frodsham in the complexity of its medieval plan rendering its townscape very diversified and producing many visual surprises.[10]

In siting, layout, visible structures and historical associations with the Scottish border, the pre-urban nucleus of the magnificent castle, the appended, partly-cobbled suburbium of Bailiffgate and the ancient parish church of St Michael combine to form the distinctive, more aristocratic northern half of the historical townscape. Its broad central street space focuses on the tall castle gate and gains greatly from the harmonious blending of medieval forms and serried rows of Georgian stone houses in ashlar.

Winding Narrowgate, providing equally effective surprise approaches to south and north,[11] leads to the medieval borough with its street system within three successive medieval plan units. A central triangle of prominent streets with characteristic cobble strips outlines the huge original market place, long since built over by market colonization, and thus provides particularly interesting views of the street forks at its apices and the reduced market in its middle, the whole supported by a compact stand of modest ashlared late-Georgian stone houses of three storeys, echoing the prosperity of the agricultural revolution and extending

Figure 2. Alnwick.
Building types and urban land utilization: A—Main road to Edinburgh; B—Main road to Newcastle; C—Alnwick Castle; D—St Michael's Church; E—Pottergate Tower; F—Georgian town hall; G—Northumberland Hall; H—Turk's Head; J—Hotspur Gate; For key to shades see Fig. 4. *Plan units*: 1—Pre-urban nucleus (medieval castle with modern modifications); 2—Medieval suburbium and St Michael's Church (street-market layout); 3—Original borough with triangular market and later alterations; 4—Medieval borough extension; 5—Line of former medieval town wall with existing gates; 6—Late- and post-medieval market colonization; 7—Post-medieval fringe belt and residential accretions (traditional components); 8—Post-medieval fringe belt and residential accretions (later components).

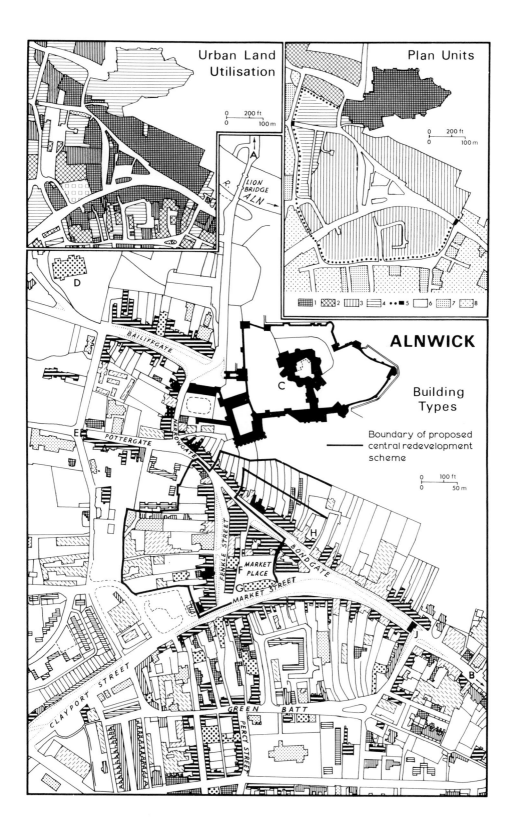

Urban Land
Utilisation

0   200 ft
0   100 m

R. ALN
LION
BRIDGE
ALN →
A

Plan Units

0   200 ft
0   100 m

1 2 3 4 5 6 7 8

D

BAILIFFGATE

NARROWGATE

C

ALNWICK

Building
Types

E

POTTERGATE

Boundary of proposed
central redevelopment
scheme

0   100 ft
0   50 m

FENKLE STREET

H

BONDGATE

F

MARKET
PLACE

G

MARKET STREET

CLAYPORT STREET

J

B

GREEN BATT

PERCY STREET

southward in the Percy Street area. A Georgian town hall, a Regency assembly hall (Northumberland Hall), the "Gothick" Pottergate Tower and the late medieval Hotspur Gate are townscape dominants strategically placed in different parts of the ancient borough. The whole ensemble typifies the old market town of the Scottish border in all its historicity.

Though the CBD has kept substantially to the central triangle, disruption of this traditional townscape by Victorian and later replacements has been slight. But the real threat is only coming now as Alnwick's geographical situation and the service requirements of modern society make the town an ideal and assured service centre for northern Northumberland. Already demolition of a prominent and interestingly featured Regency hotel (Turk's Head) is proposed to make way for a chain store, the planning authority having had to face the situation without any policy of effective townscape management. The danger is the greater as most of the late-Georgian stone houses follow the extreme self-restraint of northern classicism, are therefore not important architectural monuments individually and make the notion of their dispensability all too easy to adopt. Thus a development company has recently promoted a central redevelopment scheme which, as indicated on Fig. 2, is calculated to disrupt Alnwick's historical townscape completely. In the meantime, heavy main-road traffic continues to inflict costly damage on the fifteenth-century Hotspur Gate and John Adam's famous Lion Bridge over the Aln.

Here, then, is a clear case for townscape management on the following lines: preservation of the old town as a whole in terms of existing street spaces, continuous street fronts and not merely individual house façades; diversion of the heavy main-road traffic from the old town to a long since scheduled but still unconstructed by-pass; promotion of improvements inside the plot dominants of the central triangle in conjunction with a carefully considered scheme of possible alternative uses in preserved buildings; improvements on the burgage land behind the plot dominants along lines suggested for traditional market towns in the Buchanan Report.

Conway, though showing affinities to Frodsham in terms of its building pattern and to Alnwick and Ludlow in terms of its compositeness of plan, is nevertheless a case on its own.[12] This results from its origin by a single act of foundation as one of Edward I's Welsh bastides. It is expressed in the townscape by the castle and the town walls, a magnificent heritage even in their ruined state, and by an articulated plan of two functional units in an ingenious response to a rather complex planning problem facing the medieval planner. Castle, town gates and wall towers dominate the town silhouette and close several street vistas. Thus the fortifications tie the whole complex together into a historical townscape of strong character in spite of the unwelcome if moderate interference of the railway and the generally in-different building fabric. At least two of the few remaining pre-Georgian houses and the parish church are of considerable historical and architectural interest,[13] but prosperity after the improvement of communications (Telford's road bridge 1826, R. Stephenson's railway bridge 1848) and the development of the coast for

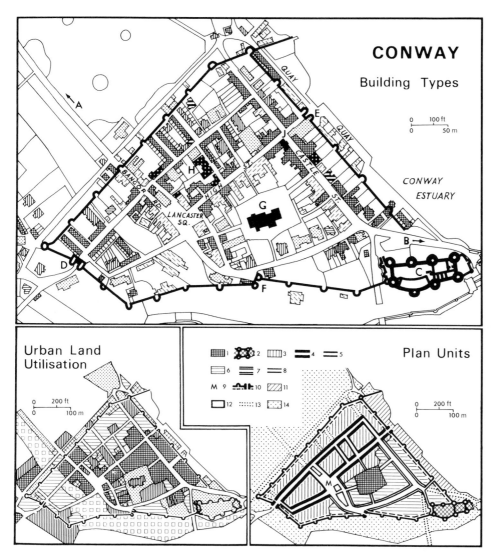

Figure 3. Conway.
Building types and urban land utilization: A—Main road to Bangor; B—Main road to Colwyn Bay; C—Conway Castle; D—Upper Gate; E—Lower Gate; F—Mill Gate; G—St Mary's Church; H—Plas Mawr (Elizabethan); J—Aberconwy (Medieval); For key to shades see Fig. 4. *Plan units*: 1—Pre-urban nucleus (Cistercian abbey and later parish church); 2—Conway Castle; 3—Parallel street system inserted between Upper and Lower Gate (4—Feeders or main streets; 5—Distributaries); 6—Meridian street system inserted between castle and parallel street system (7—Main streets; 8—Occupation lanes); 9—Market common to both systems and leading to Mill Gate; 10—Medieval town wall with gates and conjectured wall street; 11—Site of Medieval harbour; 12—Late- and post-medieval market colonization; 13—Modern streets; 14—Post-medieval fringe belt and residential accretions.

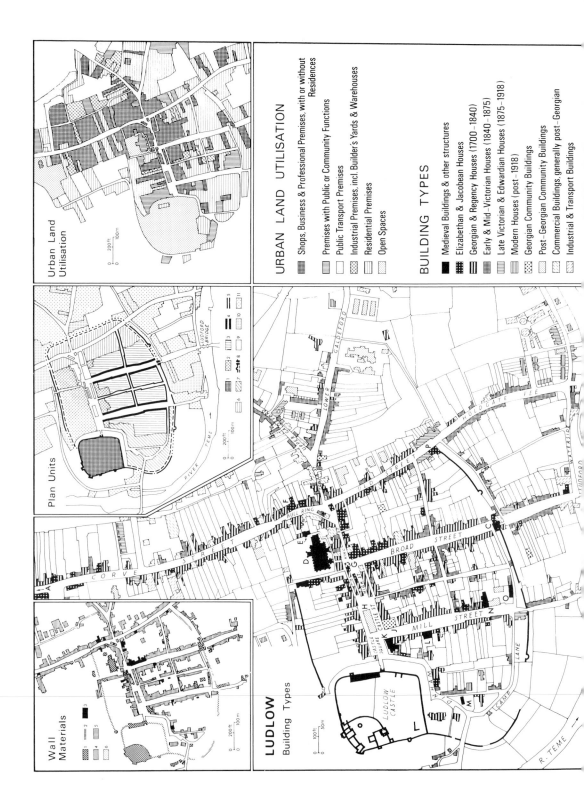

Urban Land Utilisation

200 ft
100 m
0

Plan Units

RIVER TEME
LUDFORD BRIDGE

1
2
3
4
5
6
7
8
9
10
11

200 ft
100 m
0

Wall Materials

1
2
3
4
5
6

200 ft
100 m
0

URBAN LAND UTILISATION

Shops, Business & Professional Premises, with or without Residences

Premises with Public or Community Functions

Public Transport Premises

Industrial Premises, incl. Builder's Yards & Warehouses

Residential Premises

Open Spaces

BUILDING TYPES

Medieval Buildings & other structures

Elizabethan & Jacobean Houses

Georgian & Regency Houses (1700 – 1840)

Early & Mid-Victorian Houses (1840 – 1875)

Late Victorian & Edwardian Houses (1875 – 1918)

Modern Houses (post – 1918)

Georgian Community Buildings

Post-Georgian Community Buildings

Commercial Buildings, generally post-Georgian

Industrial & Transport Buildings

LUDLOW
Building Types

100 ft
50 m
0

CORVE STREET
BULL RING
OLD STREET
KING STREET
BROAD STREET
MILL STREET
CASTLE ST
CASTLE SQUARE
LUDLOW CASTLE
LOWER GALDEFORD
GALDEFORD
HOLDGATE FEE
WHITCLIFFE
LINNEY
CAMP LANE
R. TEME

A B C D E F G H J K L M N O

tourists and retirement later account for the dominant stands of nineteenth-century building types including many commercial replacements along the re-sited main route through the town.

The main features of townscape management in Conway, then, should be as follows: the preservation of castle, town wall, parish church and the few other historic buildings and a freeing of the town walls of some of their encumberments; preservation of the identity of the medieval street system, though moderate widening of the High Street would hardly interfere with this but would not obviate the desirability of a by-pass for seasonal through-traffic; control of new building development in terms of height, scale, especially the avoidance of excessive frontage size of units in relation to the street spaces, and external materials.

Finally, Ludlow presents the most diverse and exciting townscape among all our examples, as characteristic of the Welsh border as Alnwick is of the Scottish. With Conway it has the general frame of a castle and town wall in common, though the last is not nearly so complete. But castle and Broad Gate are important townscape dominants to which must be added the tall parish church of St Lawrence with its magnificent Perpendicular tower dominating the whole town silhouette. Analogous to Alnwick, Ludlow has a genetically composite plan.[14] Like Alnwick and Whithorn, it has an overwhelmingly dominant stock of traditional buildings but of greater variety because of the prosperity of the late-Elizabethan and the Georgian periods, and there are also some medieval buildings. The fine Elizabethan timber-frame houses, some like the Feather's Hotel (1603) magnificently rich in decoration, still dominate in the north-eastern part of the walled town which forms the core of Ludlow's CBD and has very few modern commercial replacements. The larger Georgian houses have preferred the traditionally more residential western and southern parts where they form partly exclusive serried rows as they do in the formerly similar areas of Corve Street and Old Street. Post-Georgian buildings are few, the Market Hall of 1887, "Ludlow's bad luck"[15] on Castle Square, and a late-Victorian shopfront building in King

Figure 4. Ludlow.
Building types: A—Main road to Shrewsbury; B—Main road to Hereford; C—Broad Gate (13th and 18th c.); D—St Lawrence's Church (13th to 15th c.); E—Reader's House (13th, 14th and 17th c.); F—Feathers Hotel (1603); G—Butter Cross (1743–4); H—Market Hall (1887); J—Public Rooms (1840); K—Castle Lodge (14th and 16th c.); L—Guildhall (15th c. and 1768); M—St Thomas's Chapel (12th c.); N—Grammar School (14th c.); O—Barnaby House (1400); P—Town Preacher's House (1611). *Plan units*: 1—Pre-urban nucleus (Ludlow Castle); 2—Medieval suburbium (Castle Square–King St. Unit); 3—Parallel street system (Broad St.–Mill St. Unit) inserted between suburbium and Ludford river crossing (4—Main streets; 5—Occupation lanes); 6—Road convergence contemporary with suburbium, later built-up and included in walled borough (Bull Ring–Old St. Unit); 7-Residual Dinham–Camp Lane Unit; 8—Town wall with gates and conjectured wall street; 9—Late- and post-medieval market colonization; 10—Post-medieval fringe belt and residential accretions (traditional components); 11—Post-medieval fringe belt and residential accretions (later components). *Wall materials*: 1—Stone, occasionally rough-cast or partly timber frame; 2—Stone of town wall and outer castle wall; 3—Timber frame, occasionally stuccoed or rough-cast; 4—Brick, sometimes plastered or rough-cast; 5—Vertical boarding; 6—Corrugated iron sheeting.

Street being the major indiscretions. Thus the threefold contrast of medieval stone, Elizabethan black-and-white timberwork and Georgian brick is allowed to add its distinctive note to one of the most complete, richest and satisfyingly accented historical townscapes in this country.

Townscape management should treat the walled town and Corve Street as a whole, preserving the existing street spaces—including the fifteenth-century Ludford Bridge and Dinham Bridge (1823). Full preservation should also apply to all townscape dominants and to the bulk of the traditional building fabric in conjunction with a carefully prepared scheme of possible alternative uses. Heavy through traffic, already finding Ludford Bridge difficult to negotiate, needs to by-pass the old town altogether.

Conclusion

In the light of our discussion and the evidence presented by our five examples a few general points can be made finally about historical townscapes and their planning problems.

There is the fundamental fact that individual historical townscapes are unique, no two being exactly alike. This, in conjunction with their social importance and their liability to become wasting assets through mismanagement, renders the preservation of all historical townscapes an important social charge on town and country planning in a society with greatly increased physical mobility of individuals and the need for an expanding educative and cultural background.

Uniqueness of historical townscapes lies in the highly individualized spatial association of traditional urban forms, represented especially by the town plans and their street spaces, the assortment and distribution patterns of building types, and the townscape dominants. Generally, the greater the variety of plan and building forms and their spatial association, the greater the degree of uniqueness in the townscape. Larger historical towns, being usually more composite in plan and having experienced more than one historical period of prosperity, tend to exhibit a greater richness and degree of individualization in their historicity.

All our examples show the combination of a medieval plan and mainly post-medieval traditional building fabric. This represents one very widespread generic type of historical townscape, making the study of the methods of its townscape management a matter of general urgency. But there are other generic types equally worthy of immediate attention.

Though our examples are small historical towns subject so far only to moderate functional pressure in terms of central redevelopment, the functional potential of their CBDs is considerable in view of the re-emergence of these towns as sub-regional service centres. Thus their townscape management is a hardly less urgent matter than that of larger towns. Pressures on existing forms are not only those of central land utilization but also those of the associated centripetal traffic. They present distinct problems of townscape management.

As historical townscapes are liable to become wasting assets of society, their management inevitably has to emphasize preservation of traditional forms as a first priority. But this is not the whole of townscape management which must go beyond preservation to include active help in the accommodation of land and building uses within preserved traditional forms and control of new modern forms within a historical townscape. Systematic study is urgently needed in both these matters.

To be at all worthwhile preservation must recognize the spatial continuity and morphological structure of the historical townscape and must avoid any unduly restricted view of its function. It is concerned with street spaces individually and in terms of plan units, with plots and plot groupings, with building groups in terms of the whole stock of existing traditional buildings, and with individual buildings and structures of special importance.

In the preservation of traditional street spaces a fundamental point is that the bounding building façades are integral parts of the street space. Serried rows of buildings facing one another across a street space are in visual relation with one another as well as with the intervening space. When this occurs, as it usual, within the same plan unit, the rhythm of the traditional plot pattern as apparent in the plot frontages emphasizes the unity of the whole. Therefore a medieval street space bared of its peripheral buildings as a result of slum clearance and the institution of car parks loses its identity completely even though its traditional street lines may remain unchanged. Further the separate street spaces within the same plan unit are in rapport with each other and with their associated plot pattern, the more so if ancient rights of way have developed along traditional strip plots. And finally there is morphological rapport between different traditional plan units. The many architectural, engineering and planning problems of street-space and plan-unit preservation call for systematic study.

The preservation of building groups, generally though not exclusively in terms of their street façades, poses special architectural problems in the CBD. Systematic study, preferably on a comparative basis drawing on the whole of European pre- and post-war experience, is needed of the conversion of traditional buildings and the design of new buildings incorporating fully preserved and reconstituted traditional façades.

This leads to the general problem of accommodating modern land uses in the historical townscape as a whole. Here too, systematic study is urgently needed. What central or other land-use types can be architecturally accommodated in unaltered or altered traditional building types of various kinds or behind preserved façades? What are the principles of fitting a specific CBD structure into the existing form complex of a particular historical townscape so as to achieve optimum accord between them without undue sacrifice of functional efficiency? What should the associated landownership and planning policy be?

Finally, there is the question of new buildings in a historical townscape and their external architectural control. In terms of principles this is possibly a more straight-forward architectural problem resolving itself basically into the requirement of the harmonization of new buildings with surrounding traditional forms in scale, elevational rhythm and external building materials.

The geographical investigation of historical townscapes in the light of their genesis and present function provides important criteria for the recognition of specific problems and methods of townscape management and above all an emphatic reminder that the uniqueness and variety of townscapes requires great flexibility of approach on the part of the planner.

Notes

1. Ministry of Transport (1964) *Traffic in towns* (Harmondsworth). Relevant examples are those of Newbury and Norwich.

2. Bobek, H. (1948) "Stellung und Bedeutung der Sozialgeographie", *Erdkunde* 2, 122.

3. Schwind, M. (1951) "Kulturlandschaft als objektivierter Geist", *Dte geogr. Bl.* **46**, 5–28.

4. Conzen, M. R. G. (1960) *Alnwick, Northumberland: a study in town-plan analysis* Inst. Br. Geogr. Publ. No. 27.

5. Some discussion of recurrent urban building types in Britain, with illustrations, can be found in Conzen, M. R. G. (1958) "The growth and character of Whitby", in Daysh, G. H. J. (ed.) *A survey of Whitby and the surrounding area* (Eton) pp. 49–89, but the subject awaits exhaustive treatment from the geographical viewpoint.

6. For this reason only plot dominants are shown on the main maps in Figs 1–4.

7. The maps are based on field surveys carried out by the author at various times during the period 1945 to 1964.

8. Stewart, D. M. (1948) "The architecture of the 'Machars' district of Galloway", *Q. Jl R. Inc. Archit. Scot.* **71**, 14–30.

9. Ormerod, G. (1882) *The history of the county palatine and city of Chester*, Vol. 2, 2nd edn (London) pp. 46–61; Beamont, W. (1881) *An account of the ancient town of Frodsham in Cheshire* (Warrington).

10. Tate, G. (1868–9) *The history of the borough, castle and barony of Alnwick*, 2 vols (Alnwick); Conzen (1960) op. cit. (note 4).

11. Pevsner, N. (1957) *Northumberland* (Harmondsworth) p. 74.

12. Lewis, E. A. (1912) *The medieval boroughs of Snowdonia* (n.p.); Toy, S. (1936) "The town and castle of Conway", *Archaeologia* **86**, 163–93; Jones, W. G. and Fox, C. (1937) "The castle and borough of Conway", *Archaeologia Cambrensis* **92**, 365–7; Hughes, H. H. (1938) "The Edwardian castle and town defences of Conway", *Archaeologia Cambrensis* **93**, 75, 212; Hemp, W. J. (1941) "Conway castle", *Archaeologia Cambrensis* **96**, 163–74.

13. Hughes, H. H. (1935) "Aberconwy, Conway", *Archaeologia Cambrensis* **90**, 148–51; Jones, W. G. (1937) "Plas Mawr, Conway", *Archaeologia Cambrensis* **92**, 367–70; Baker, A. and H. (1888) Plas Mawr (London); Jones, W. G. (1937) "Conway church", *Archaeologia Cambrensis* **92**, 370–2.

14. Contrary to the view of Hope, W. H. S. (1909) "The ancient topography of Ludlow", *Archaeologia* **61**, 383–9, reiterated in Wood, P. D. (1962) "Frontier relics in the Welsh border towns", *Geography* **47**, 61. The plan units are (1) the castle (pre-urban nucleus), (2) the Castle Square–King Street unit (suburbium), (3) the Bull Ring–Old Street unit, (4) the Broad Street–Mill Street unit, (5) the Dinham–Camp Lane unit.

15. Pevsner, N. (1958) *Shropshire* (Harmondsworth) p. 188.

FOUR

Geography and townscape conservation*

M. R. G. CONZEN

Modern urbanization is increasing the importance of townscapes as the physical environment of a growing proportion of mankind, particularly in economically advanced countries. Adequate townscape management, including conservation and development, is therefore an important social task of spatial planning. It is endangered by environmental attitudes of modern society tending to unqualified preference accorded to material and economic goals, to the neglect of basic cultural and spiritual needs. It is also imperilled by insufficiencies in town planning itself, often resulting in a rudimentary conception of comprehensive planning and a limited sectional but in practice dominant approach by some planners trained as surveyors or road engineers. All these tendencies are aggravated by the enormous scale and indiscriminate use of modern building technology, involving the loss of human scale in townscape creation, and by the "facelessness" of much contemporary architecture. Among big cities with a high rate of physical change this produces increasingly anonymous uniformity. Historical townscapes, a valuable, widespread and particularly vulnerable kind of environmental asset in Europe, face special dangers in this respect and call for forms of management directed more specifically towards townscape conservation.

To achieve optimal management of the physical environment on behalf of society planning must effect a well considered balance between many different and often conflicting claims of society on environmental space and for that purpose must view that space as a whole. Geography, as the discipline concerned with the nature of the geosphere, also adopts a holistic view of the same space and should be particularly suited to providing planning with an appropriate spatial approach, urban geography in this context being relevant to town planning.

Urban geography, however, though looking back on a history of some 75 years, is still a developing subject. For the last 40 years it has been much preoccupied

* First published in "Anglo-German Symposium in Applied Geography, Giessen-Würzburg-München, 1973", *Giessener Geographische Schriften* 1975, pp. 95–102. Reprinted by permission of Professor Dr H. Uhlig.

with the important functional aspect of towns, and any holistic view of the town as a geographical phenomenon has been somewhat impeded by the relative neglect of the genetic-developmental and morphological aspects, some notable exceptions in the literature notwithstanding. Not unexpectedly, urban land utilization is one aspect of the townscape that has found more attention from functionally orientated urban geographers. However, quantitative methods developed in the historically simpler and more uniform situation of North America and approaching the analysis of the townscape with the notion of critical threshold values for various functional attributes, as in the investigation of American central business districts, are insufficient if not to say inappropriate in the very different situation of Europe, the area of historical townscapes *par excellence*. Here genetically informed observation of morphological elements, orientated towards the spatial structure of the whole townscape and not merely its land utilization aspect, is an essential prerequisite for understanding the character of the townscape and thus providing a rational basis for successful townscape management.

Historically conditioned townscapes, however, are very complicated objects in terms of spatial structure and systematic contents, and it is not surprising that the few monographic studies in recent urban morphology have tended to emphasize particular aspects of the subject or else the individuality of particular cases rather than their potential contribution to a comprehensive general theory of the townscape. Klöpper's study of the centre of Mainz, for example, concentrates on the functional aspect of the townscape with the aim of identifying "town quarters" by classifying and mapping land-use elements on the basis of their inherent functional location requirements.[1] Two studies from North England focus on the town plan, presenting the structure of the townscape in terms of morphogenetic plan units based on the identification of formative processes, and aiming at the development of general concepts based on the systematic observation of plan elements.[2] The extensive, diversified and detailed study of Vienna by Bobek and Lichtenberger emphasizes the building fabric, producing a genetic typology of building types and their spatial associations and resulting in the analysis of townscape structure in terms of historically and functionally conditioned "building-fabric regions".[3]

These and other investigations show awareness of the connections that exist between different systematic facets of the townscape and between the morphological and other aspects of urban geography. But so far we have achieved neither comprehensiveness nor balance in the study of the townscape as a whole, and there is no established body of general concepts covering all aspects of the townscape to facilitate comparative study over wider areas. Because of their time depth, historical dynamism and variety of formative processes the historical townscapes of Europe represent a particularly important field of enquiry in this respect. As indicated earlier, they are also of special interest to, and provide crucial material for, the development of any consolidated theory of townscape management and conservation. As it is, there is as yet no comprehensive theory of urban morphology capable of offering a conceptual basis for application to planning practice.

As a contribution to the solution of this problem it is proposed here to re-introduce the general notion of urban morphology as an integral part of urban geography and as a prerequisite to townscape conservation. Some aspects of the townscape as a geographical phenomenon are discussed, more particularly with reference to the historical townscape, and some implications for society and for townscape conservation are suggested.

The townscape in urban geography

In the light of the modern theory of regions (*Landschaftslehre*)[4] towns must be regarded as distinct spatial individuals or regions. As such they have four fundamental attributes which provide the basis of four separate though frequently combined research approaches.

First, towns represent discrete spatial integrations of a variety of forces and factors in nature and human society. They are thus open functional systems in space, albeit orientated towards, and dominated by, the needs of human society as these develop and change through time. The geographically effective carrier of the human or social complex in any particular town is the urban society of that town, that is the locally fixed socio-geographical group in Bobek's sense,[5] creating and using the town as its habitat and/or work-place and so functioning as a geographically discrete yet integral part of society at large within a particular cultural and environmental context. Geographical investigation directed towards this aspect of urban geography represents the functional approach.

Secondly, though essentially spatial phenomena to the geographer, towns exist also in time, involving continuity and change within the whole context of open systems in the four-dimensional continuum of the geosphere. Thus they experience temporal development which influences their geographical character through its different phases, cultural and regional facies, and changing stages of regional integration. Such influence manifests itself in the traditions, attitudes and actions of the inhabitants of a town, and in the many relict forms of its townscape. All this belongs to the historico-geographical approach in urban geography.

Thirdly, representing individualized spatial systems within the geosphere, towns carry uniqueness as one of their basic attributes. In this respect they become objects of idiographic or regional study. Yet the fact that all these systems draw on the geosphere as their common reservoir of forces and factors means that their uniqueness is not "random" or unrelated but that they are capable of sharing characteristics of various kinds and in varying degree. They are therefore susceptible to comparative regional study. Both forms of investigation, the idiographic and the comparative, are found in what can be termed the regional approach.

Last but not least, towns possess material form. Commensurate with their functional significance within the world's ecosystem they present a distinctive kind of cultural landscape, the urban landscape or townscape. Its investigation is the object of the morphological approach. Compared with other types of cultural landscape the townscape is characterized by greater morphological intensity. Man-made form elements in several systematically distinct form complexes occur in greater variety and at higher distribution density within the urban built-up area. In part this results from the degree of intricacy in functional structure combined with the corollary of size. Generally speaking greater functional significance of a town will produce greater morphological diversity. The functional structure of the town will be reflected in its morphological structure. However, by itself present function will not account for the character of a townscape except in the few cases of new towns or of towns in which there has been radical replacement of inherited forms. The great majority of towns have a history of some duration reflected in the townscape by relict forms which are more extensive than is commonly assumed. Their variety depends on the length and accidents of history in each case and not only enhances the morphological diversity of the townscape but commonly forms a major aspect of the town's geographical personality.

Within their regional setting, then, urban settlements provide culmination points or areas of the cultural landscape as much as of the functional web of human activities. As the four basic attributes of the town are integrated so that each of them is influenced by the other three, it is not surprising to find that the townscape expresses the functional life of the town and its society in the present, reflects that of the past, and portrays the time-conditioned identity or personality of the town.

Complexity characterizes the structure of the townscape in two respects, systematically in terms of the different kinds of contents or form elements and spatially in terms of the way these form elements are associated in space as the result of historical development and functional requirements. The former represents the static, the latter the dynamic aspect of the townscape.

Each of the three systematic form complexes (town plan, building fabric, and urban land utilization pattern) is made up of several kinds of form elements. Thus the town plan consists of streets or other communication spaces, land parcels or plots, and the block-plans of individual buildings which form the corresponding plan-element complexes of street system, plot pattern, and building pattern. The design of any particular plan element or group of elements, such as a medieval street space or combination of street spaces, a series of plots for Victorian working-class housing, or a pair of modern semi-detached houses, is determined by two criteria—original functional purpose and period of origin. Combined these provide a basis for a morphogenetic classification of plan elements appropriate to geographical plan analysis.

Similarly the building fabric has individual buildings as its constituent form elements. These are classified morphogenetically by the same twin criteria, the original purposes of buildings forming systematic element complexes such as dwelling-houses, commercial buildings, industrial buildings, and community buildings. Within each of these element complexes period divisions produce historical type groups, such as the Georgian, the early- and mid-Victorian, or the late-Victorian and Edwardian in Britain. These in turn are subdivided morpho-genetically into actual building types on the basis of their design for a particular purpose within a definite period context resulting in specific characteristics of plan, elevation and architectural style. Period classification is commonly used in the typology of dwelling-houses but is geographically just as necessary in the case of non-residential buildings,[6] a point often overlooked. To be geographically significant, however, the period classification of buildings must relate directly or indirectly to the formative processes of socio-economic history responsible for the creation of the building types. Therefore period designations in terms of purely architectural style history, as used in the early work of Hassinger[7] and Schaefer[8] are geographically significant only if they relate to changes in socio-economic history.

In contrast to town plan and building fabric the elements of the urban land utilization pattern, that is the individual units of land utilization occupying discrete plots, do not depend fundamentally on the period of origin for their classification even though their location and the pattern as a whole needs to be understood in developmental terms. Classification can therefore be based on the single criterion of purpose. Element complexes are represented by major functional categories such as residential, commercial, industrial, or community service functions and their subdivision produces the detailed classification of actual land-use types. These last segregate or combine variously in the townscape to form different local groupings of functional significance, thus making up the functional structure of the townscape.

In purely static terms the physical combination of town plan, building fabric and land utilization pattern occurs in a somewhat hierarchical manner whereby the town plan "contains", and forms the general frame of, the land utilization pattern, and the land-use units or plots in turn "contain" the building fabric. In this way the three form complexes together with the natural substratum of the site combine locally to produce the smallest, morphologically homogeneous areas provisionally termed "townscape cells". In a variety of ways which need further investigation these townscape cells group themselves into minor townscape units which in turn combine at different levels of integration to form a hierarchy of intra-urban regions. Complexity of spatial structure is already engendered by the articulation of each of the three systematic distribution patterns and is increased by the fact that these patterns are not conformable. Clearly the townscape cannot be comprehended in static terms but must be seen as the result of dynamic processes originating in urban society in its wider social and regional context and operating through time. Historical townscapes would seem to hold the best clue to such understanding.

The historical townscape

Reference has been made to the society of a town as the socio-geographical group responsible for the existence of the town. It is essentially a "settlement group" or a spatially defined social complex, diversified in its internal structure and operating as an integral part of a wider social system of cultural, economic and political complexion.[9] The town is its immediate habitat and owes its morphology to the functional requirements of that society. As these requirements change in the course of time so do the forms designed to cater for them, namely types of town plan, urban building types, and the location of particular types of urban land use. These morphological changes are not random but correspond to periods of socio-economic and cultural history which manifest themselves in the townscape as morphological periods, each with its own set of distinctive forms. Complete, let alone instant, substitution of outmoded or obsolescent forms by new ones is rare in urban history, though periods of economic prosperity and associated building booms have usually resulted in a greater amount of building replacement. Generally, however, relict forms from different periods survive in the shape of buildings and large parts of the town plan and give rise to historical layering in the townscape. Surviving lineaments of an earlier plan act widely as morphological frames for subsequent development (Fig. 1).

Thus accumulation of relict forms through time becomes one of the fundamental morphological processes of the landscape and in that general sense renders most townscapes historical. It also imparts a kind of resistant separateness to the townscape vis-à-vis its occupant society, increasing the discordance between current functional requirements and inherited townscape equipment. The effort of society to overcome this discordance results in further morphological processes, namely the adaptation and transformation of historical forms or else their replacement by new forms.

The diversity of morphological processes makes the townscape more complex and this effect is substantially increased by the differential time response of town plan, building fabric and land-use pattern to changing functional needs. Town plan and to a lesser extent building fabric are conservative in that they tend to reflect the pattern of past landownership and capital investment longer. Therefore they present a greater range and quantity of traditional forms (those dating from before 1840–50) and thus contribute substantially to the historical character of the townscape. The land-use pattern responds more easily to changing functional impulses, its influence on an historical townscape being therefore more negative. These complications of dynamic morphology diversify the modes of spatial form association in different parts of the town according to the functional potential and particular circumstances of localities in different periods. The result is complexity in the structure of individual form associations as well as in the general pattern of these associations. Thus a medieval English "high-street" plan with narrow strip plots (burgages) may be occupied conformably by Georgian dwelling-houses now used entirely for commercial and professional purposes while neighbouring localities may show element mixtures of different historical time range and degree of internal conformability. Morphological processes especially characteristic of particular parts of Europe, for example in Britain the burgage cycle of building repletion and clearance, and certain standard modes of replacement within

Figure 1.

pre-existing morphological frames increase the complexity, variety and interest of historical townscapes.

In this way historical townscapes obtain their individualized local structures in terms of smallest coherent form associations or townscape cells combining to form minor, medium and major townscape units and ultimately the town as a whole (Fig. 1). At all these levels of integration respective units display among other characteristics those of uniqueness and developmental or historical significance. This last might be expressed in many different ways ranging from the rich historical layering often found in the "Old Town" centres of historical cities to the contemporaneous homogeneity of more recent peripheral areas. Thus different towns and indeed their different parts vary in what we can call their historical expressiveness or historicity. A concomitant though not necessarily dependent attribute is that of their aesthetic significance.

As form after form is added to an already existing townscape by its occupant urban society in the course of history, only some of these forms replacing earlier ones, the whole townscape becomes the "objectivation of the spirit"[10] of that society in its broader culture context and in the context of its own historical development on a particular town site. That objectivation is best shown by the historical townscape as a whole but also finds varying partial expression in its regional subdivisions. In either case it is individualized in the form of groupings on the ground and their articulation by layout or by dominant forms such as prominent buildings. Objectivation of the spirit becomes the spirit of the place or the *genius loci*, which represents an important environmental experience for the individual even when it is received more or less unconsciously. In the physical arrangement of the townscape then, the objectivation of the spirit finds its particularized form or *gestalt* and affects the individual in three ways. At the practical everyday level it is necessary for independent orientation within the townscape, our mental map of the town depending on our functional experience of the identity of localities within it as perception studies have confirmed.[11] At the aesthetic level we add an equally spontaneous emotional dimension to that experience, and at the intellectual level, depending on the individual's mental access to relevant information, we experience the townscape in its full socio-cultural context well beyond the confines of the individual town or the present time.

Historicity is an important ingredient in this compound experience. Even in famous historical towns, particularly the larger ones, historicity is unevenly distributed within the town area, its intensity commonly culminating in the Old Town and perhaps in association with certain morphological frames or particular historical complexes outside it. This raises the question of the assessment of townscape historicity, which has a bearing on conservation procedure, especially the establishment of priorities. A quantitative approach to this subject may be impossible, but it might be useful to mention likely criteria for assessment. The first would appear to be the historical time range and the incidence of mor-phological periods represented in the townscape as a whole and within each of the three systematic form complexes. Secondly, there is the spatial incidence and distribution pattern of historical forms within one systematic form complex, including their degree of spatial admixture and concentration. Thirdly, we have the diverse local association and degree of mutual conformability of the three systematic form complexes. Thus the ensemble of a row of independently designed Tudor, Jacobean, and perhaps Georgian town houses conformably occupying a series of narrow medieval (8·5 m) burgage plots flanking a medieval English market-place has a historicity value different from that of a case where such an arrangement has been partially disrupted by modern burgage amalgamation associated with building replacement by modern chain or department stores. Fourthly, the degree of historicity can be affected by the obsolescence and structural decay of forms, and fifthly, historicity is affected by site circumstances including adjacent land-use context and landscape setting.

One final general point concerns the distribution of historical townscapes. As most towns need some time to develop they are in a sense all historical, and it is not straining the term too much to say that historical townscapes with a development of more than 200 years occur in most parts of the world. But strong historicity in a townscape depends not only on the time depth but also the diversity and dynamism of its associated urban history, including in particular the strength of urban institutions and cultural traditions. In this respect Europe is an area of exceptional interest with a long if varied experience of comparatively free urban societies. Europe also excels in considerable regional variation and in the spread and diversifying effect of repeated innovations in its urban history. Not surprisingly, historians interested in the institutional aspects of urban development have been able to identify many contrasting distribution areas in this respect, so-called *Städtelandschaften* originating in the Middle Ages, a great formative period in European town life.

Society, townscape conservation and geography

Three basic questions are posed by the problem of townscape conservation. What is the social purpose of conservation? What are the dangers threatening the conservation of historical townscapes in Europe? What is the general nature of conservation? We shall try to discuss some of these questions.

That historical townscapes serve an important social purpose and that their progressive effacement represents an irreparable cultural loss to the community has been directly or indirectly acknowledged by modern society in the repeated attempts to recreate a destroyed historical townscape in the subsequent re-development of its site. The Rows of Chester are one of the better known early examples of this century and there have been many more in continental Europe in the period since World War II. The steadily increasing scope of governmental as well as voluntary conservation activities at the present time points in the same direction. But it is perhaps not so easy to define the social purpose of conservation more specifically in terms of the value which historical townscapes have for society. What we have said about their value to the individual in the previous section might be expanded usefully. Society or any of its groupings, such as the urban society as a settlement group, derive benefit from the historical townscape in a threefold way: by its utility, its aesthetic quality, and its intellectual value. In practice the last two of these are not easy to separate. In any case culture-conscious individuals and social groups will always tend to integrate all three in their experience.

It is suggested that historical townscapes have the highest intellectual value among all townscapes. An urban environment of strong historicity is an important asset to any healthy and expanding form of social life at advanced levels of civilization. It engenders a sense of continuity and diversity of human effort and achievement at different periods, a "tradition" in a wider rather than any narrow sense. It enables the social mind as much as that of the individual to take root in an area through the depth of time perspective and the sense of group-supported continuity which it adds to the awareness of one's own social existence on the ground. This is one prerequisite for any balanced relation between individual and society and between the urban society and its habitat. Through its higher urban distribution density of man-made forms an historical townscape imparts a stronger visual experience of historical layering, and in demonstrating the historical dimension of human experience stimulates comparison and thus a more informed way of reasoning. The effect of this is intensified by the *gestalt*-wise manifestation of historicity in different intra-urban localities and is multiplied in regions with a diversity of historical townscapes, stimulating as these are in their unending variations on the theme of the *genius loci*. Thus historical townscapes exercise an educative and regenerative influence on the mind which answers a fundamental long-term social requirement.

All this implies not only that the conservation of historical townscapes is an important cultural requirement of society at large but that knowledge about these townscapes and their spatial structure is needed not only for scholarly reasons but also for practical purposes. Here then is a field awaiting the urban morphologist and requiring the development of a coherent body of concepts explaining townscapes in terms of their spatial development and structure, a morphogenetic theory of towns.

Aesthetic quality is the second socially relevant aspect of historical townscapes in that it supports the emotive function of the environment needed by society. Direct aesthetic reference is present in several characteristics of the historical townscape, such as the preservation of the human scale in its traditional form complexes or the compositeness of medieval town plans. This results in visually interesting and satisfying asymmetric arrangements of parts with eccentrically located townscape dominants, visual surprises in the sequence of narrow streets and open squares, emphasis of particular points and altogether an aesthetic ease of orientation by uniquely placed "landmarks". Contrasts of forms recall old functional differences such as that between market-place and cathedral close. The harmony established between conformable form complexes of different period provenance gives a sense of continuity of successful human aspirations in the context of a closely-knit community firmly rooted in its inherited habitat. As these examples show, at every turn the aesthetic aspect is liable to intertwine with the intellectual one. Here too spatially orientated morphogenetic analysis is relevant.

Further there is the aspect of utility which has already been touched upon earlier. By their very nature historical townscapes are liable to encounter greater discordance between current functional requirements and inherited forms. The old solution of simply destroying the inherited form by replacement under the absolute primacy of economic considerations is gradually giving way to more informed attitudes often already enjoying official support and aiming successfully at the conservation of inherited forms by accommodating new concordant functions in them in conditions in which continuing diversification of urban functions has increased the prospects of conservation by concordant change. Though these problems are supposed to lie more clearly within the professional sphere of the town planner, at any rate in Britain, it would appear that here too the analytical work of the urban geographer could find a fruitful field.

In any case there seems as yet to be no guarantee anywhere in Europe that the mere presence of planning organs already safeguards historical townscapes. Economic pressure on these townscapes is commonly greatest just where their historicity is strongest—in the Old Town kernels which are now the main commercial and business cores. Additional dangers come from some of the town planners themselves who approach the planning of their cities with narrow sectional bias in favour of a type of road planning which has already been recognized as outdated and is liable to destroy the identity of historical townscapes irretrievably, especially under the application of modern constructional and transport technology. Ultimately the greatest danger is liable to come from society itself. In a democratic society the state of the cultural landscape and in particular the preservation or neglect of its historicity reflects fairly closely the average cultural consciousness of that society and so indirectly the long-term efficiency of its education system. Changes in the life style of modern society are bringing increasing depersonalization in work and education, greater emphasis on the satisfaction of material requirements and increasing loss of the sense of historical and cultural continuity even though the modern mass media and increased personal mobility are potentially widening the range and variety of cultural experiences. Thus an historically charged and varied environment for daily and periodic enjoyment is of great importance, and historical townscapes play a significant role, especially if they are available at relatively high distribution density.

This is not the place to go into the technicalities of townscape conservation but a list of its various facets may help to indicate the relevance of geographical work to it. There is: (1) conservation of the physiognomic identity of the historical town as a whole and of its constituent parts, which involves the establishment of spatial units of conservation, (2) conservation of historicity as a corollary of identity, (3) conservation and enhancement of aesthetic quality to the same end, (4) conservation of the intelligibility of the historical townscape for the purpose of orientation on the ground, (5) preservation of the human scale, (6) functional control and management of the building fabric by functional continuation, adaptation and concordant change, (7) structural control and management of the building fabric by maintenance, restoration, internal renovation, concordant replacement and small-scale redevelopment, (8) conservative control of street-spaces and the street-system, and concordant traffic planning control.

In the execution of these tasks the most important contribution of geographical townscape analysis lies in the identification of constituent townscape units (regions) and the type and intensity of their historicity, since these aspects affect the majority of the tasks listed.

Notes

1. Klöpper, R. (1962) "Der Stadtkern als Stadtteil: ein methodologischer Versuch zur Abgrenzung und Stufung von Stadtteilen am Beispiel von Mainz", in Norborg, K. (ed.) *Proceedings of the IGU symposium in urban geography Lund 1960* (Lund) pp. 535–53.

2. See Chapter 2 and Conzen, M. R. G. (1960) *Alnwick, Northumberland: a study in town-plan analysis* Inst. Br. Geogr. Publ. No. 27.

3. Bobek, H. and Lichtenberger, E. (1966) *Wien: Bauliche Gestalt und Entwicklung seit der Mitte des 19. Jahrhunderts* (Graz).

4. Neef, E. (1967) *Die theoretischen Grundlagen der Landschaftslehre* (Gotha).

5. Bobek, H. (1948) "Stellung und Bedeutung der Sozialgeographie", *Erdkunde* 2, p. 122; Bobek, H. (1949) "Aufriss einer vergleichenden Sozialgeographie", *Mitt. geogr. Ges. Wien* **91**, 34–45.

6. Conzen, M. R. G. (1958) "The growth and character of Whitby", in Daysh, G. H. J. (ed.) *A survey of Whitby and the surrounding area* (Eton) pp. 49–89.

7. Hassinger, H. (1916) *Kunsthistorischer Atlas von Wien Österreichische Kunsttopographie 15* (Vienna).

8. Schaefer, G. (1929) *Kunstgeographischer Plan der Stadt Basel* (Basel).

9. Bobek (1948, 1949) op. cit. (note 5).

10. Schwind, M. (1951) "Kulturlandschaft als objektivierter Geist", *Dte geogr. Bl.* **46**, 5–28. See also Schwind, M. (1964) *Kulturlandschaft als geformter Geist* (Darmstadt).

11. Lynch, K. (1960) *The image of the city* (Cambridge, Mass.).

FIVE

The morphology of towns in Britain during the industrial era*

M. R. G. CONZEN

The town as a spatial phenomenon poses an immediate environmental problem for an ever increasing proportion of mankind. This is particularly true of Europe, rich as it is in towns and in the long experience of an historically and regionally diversified urban tradition. Here, urban people frequently represent a high percentage of the total population. In Britain, for example, where industrialization began in an historical context that included a broad base of medieval urban foundations, more than 80 per cent of the population is urban.

The urban resident experiences the town in its spatial dimension above all as a functionally diversified community fixed in a particular settlement and having a special importance within society as a whole. It represents a localized socio-geographical complex, or in Bobek's term a "local society" (*Lokalgesellschaft*)[1] with a distinct urban mode of life. In this the individual plays some functional role, regardless of whether the community is small enough to allow him comprehensive personal contacts within it or so large that his limited contacts are enveloped within the general anonymity of city life.

But we experience the town also in another and spiritually enriching dimension. Because this functional community is fixed in its place as a "local society", it transforms its settlement according to its diverse needs, not once but continuously in the course of history. Its requirements, its aspirations, its ideas, its entire "personality", along with those of its constituent groups and individuals, are objectivated on the earth's surface[2] as an ensemble of different and variously associated material forms that we perceive as the face of the town, as the visible townscape (*Stadtlandschaft, paysage urbain*). The townscape is the morphological expression of urban life in its local uniqueness and historical unfolding. Not only is

* First published in Jäger, H. (ed.) (1978) *Probleme des Städtewesens im industriellen Zeitalter* (Cologne) pp. 1–48. This version is based on an initial translation from the German by Kathleen Neils Conzen and Michael P. Conzen with minor revisions by the author and is reprinted by permission of Böhlau Verlag GmbH, Cologne.

it an undeniable part of our daily environment but it also offers us an evolutionary clue to, and thus deeper insight into, the local urban society. In addition we may identify with the townscape in a social, aesthetic, or some other sense, according to the type of town and our personal disposition.

Urban society, urban life, and townscape, therefore, form a unity in space despite, or rather because of, the constant tension between society and landscape. This tension results from the differential persistence of landscape matter in the face of the ever changing needs of society, thus creating in urban society a continual awareness and consequent re-evaluation of its spatial existence.

The townscape as a morphological phenomenon has been of interest to several disciplines concerned with the town, not only planners and architects but also such scholars as historians and geographers. For all of them the townscape is first of all an important document of urban genesis and development, but a document written upon repeatedly—a palimpsest[3] that can often be deciphered only through intensive investigation of the stock of extant landscape forms. The need for such morphological analysis arises from the differences in the resistance of town plan, building fabric, and land and building utilization to the pressure of changing functional needs, which create an apparent confusion in the forms belonging to different historical periods, particularly in the city centre.

This paper concerns the British townscape, its formation and transformation during the era of industrialization. The unique circumstances of Britain in the eighteenth and nineteenth centuries produced unprecedented expansion and refashioning of its existing townscapes as well as the creation of entirely new ones. In order to understand the principal morphological processes involved in these transformations, it is necessary to consider the social and historical context of Britain's industrial revolution.

Britain during the era of industrialization[4]

Although some technical, economic, and social preconditions for modern industrialization existed before the rate of industrial development began to accelerate noticeably, that is prior to 1760, its actual development belongs to the second half of the eighteenth century and the entire nineteenth century. Its historical foundation rests upon the relatively independent medieval and early modern social, economic, and cultural development of a comparatively protected island country at the Atlantic terminus of the great cultural main route from Italy and the Mediterranean to the Netherlands and the open oceans.

Important facets of this foundation include the early transition from a raw wool export economy to a self-processing one, the increasing variety of craft activities, relative proximity to the sea of nearly all important regions and centres of production, and an innovation potential in the population that promised well not only for agricultural improvement but also for mechanical developments in industry. Also relevant are the definitive political union in the early part of the eighteenth century, the emergence of a form of government conducive to the growth of an unbridled industrial-capitalist economy suitable for manipulation by those well-endowed with capital, and the early steps towards what would later become Britain's world-wide colonial empire.

This major process—the so-called "industrial revolution"—was characterized from the outset by technological innovation, and soon also by intensive capital investment and continuous economic growth. In the course of the first 80 years or so this gave rise to a robust form of business ethics based on the fictitious notion of the general progress of all through the unlimited competition of individuals for the surplus value or profit, the principle of *laissez-faire*. The application of capital and productive skills to mass production led to rapidly accelerating production rates and, combined with other factors, to unprecedented population growth. But it dissolved the pre-industrial economic ties within English society and substituted increasingly sharp class differences between those who possessed the new means of production and capital and those who had only their labour to offer on the open market.

The course of industrialization was aided during the first 100 years by the skilful market orientation and increased productivity of agriculture, which freed surplus labour for industry. More important were major transport improvements for the exchange of goods, people, and information. These conditions promoted a rapid integration of economic life which soon extended beyond the national boundaries and those of the British colonial empire to make Britain within a few decades the "workshop of the world".

All this caused considerable changes in the cultural landscape, among the most notable being the enormous expansion and simultaneous internal concentration of towns, as well as the creation of quite new and functionally specialized types of towns. Only slowly did the resulting serious social ills, accentuated by epidemics, lead to modifications of the *laissez-faire* principle. New public health and building legislation, progressing by stages, caused corresponding changes in the townscape, its minimum requirements predictably becoming the actual standard for most urban housing, particularly after the consolidating Public Health Act of 1875.

For summary purposes the industrial era may be divided into three phases: first, a great growth phase from the expansion of canal building and iron smelting with coke around 1760 to the effective beginning of the railway era around 1840; secondly, a phase of expansion and maturation lasting to the onset of the so-called great depression of 1873–96; and thirdly, a phase of marked deceleration in the annual growth of industrial productivity up to the beginning of the First World War.

Population developments[5]

The main population trend during the entire period was an accelerating growth rate which only began to abate during the 1880s: the population was about 6·5 m. in 1750, 10·5 m. in 1801, 16·3 m. in 1831, 23·1 m. in 1861, 33 m. in 1891, and 40·8

m. in 1911. More important for present purposes was the simultaneous urbanization of the population. At first slower than overall population growth, the rate of
urbanization increased substantially during the period, finally becoming the
dominant force in population dynamics. Rural to urban migration played a major
role in urbanization, as did periodic immigration from abroad (particularly after
the great Irish potato famine of 1845–47) and the balance between continuing high
birth rates and slowly declining death rates following the cholera epidemics of the
mid-nineteenth century. Whereas the proportion of urban residents in the total
population stood at 20 per cent in 1770 and did not reach 22 per cent until 1801, it
climbed rapidly to 50 per cent by 1851, 65 per cent by 1870, and in reaching 78 per
cent in 1911 had virtually reversed the 1801 percentages.[6]

At the same time the geographical distribution of population changed from a
relatively uniform pre-industrial pattern to the highly irregular and accentuated
distribution of 1900. At the beginning of the period a zone of slightly higher
density characterized the old grain and wool districts from the Bristol Channel to
East Anglia, and in addition there were modest concentrations in the six largest
cities. London around 1750 had about 675,000 inhabitants, and Norwich, York,
Bristol, Newcastle, and Exeter had between 10000 and 20000 inhabitants each.
By the end of the period particularly high densities existed in London, the
coalfields with their urban clusters and conurbations, and the main ports and
seaside resorts. This later picture, already incipient in 1800, had developed more
clearly by 1850, by which time only the later phenomenal areal expansion of the
towns and the addition of a number of seaside resorts was needed to complete the
modern picture.

Economy, society, and urban development[7]

The historical developments outlined so far were further complicated by the
increasing differentiation of economic life in terms of production, occupational
structure, and social stratification by income groups. Simultaneously there was a
geographical re-sorting of various types of production and services. Industries
differed in their needs and hence their preferred locations. Some located in certain
regions, such as the coalfields, the coasts and tidal estuaries. A number of
industries now making the transition from craft to factory system located in
particular towns with traditionally specialized labour. Industries with market
locations formed a mixed group in large cities, particularly in central places of the
highest rank, segregating inside these cities according to the quarter that they
preferred. This spatial re-organization and the gradual functional integration of
the whole country was facilitated considerably by improvements in transport,
initially by extensive construction of canals and turnpike roads and from about
1840 by the even more energetic building of railways.

Such changes had profound effects upon the development of towns in Britain.
The range of functional town types expanded considerably. Although a new
industry or service sometimes attached itself to an existing settlement, often

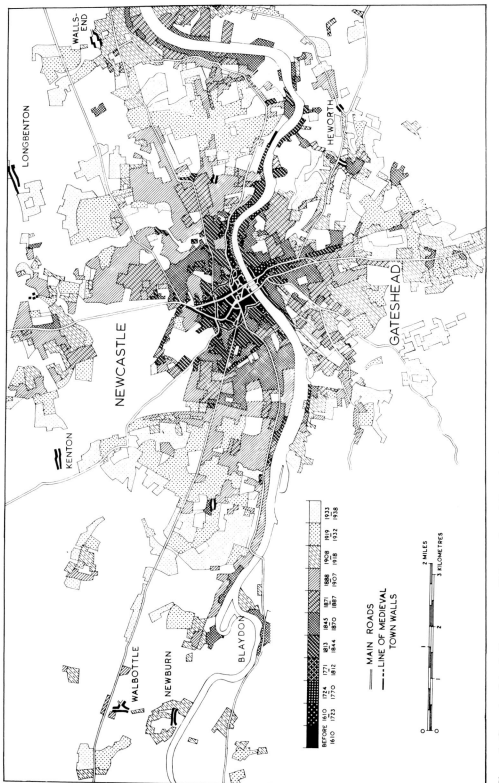

WALLS-
END

LONGBENTON

HEWORTH

NEWCASTLE

GATESHEAD

KENTON

WALBOTTLE

NEWBURN

BLAYDON

| BEFORE 1610 | 1610 1723 | 1724 1770 | 1771 1812 | 1813 1844 | 1845 1870 | 1871 1887 | 1888 1907 | 1908 1918 | 1919 1932 | 1933 1938 |

MAIN ROADS

LINE OF MEDIEVAL
TOWN WALLS

2 MILES

3 KILOMETRES

0   1   2

Figure 1. Growth of the built-up area of Newcastle and Gateshead, 1610–1918. Based on various cartographic sources.

entirely new towns grew up specializing in a single industry or service. To this class belong mining towns, iron and steel towns, railway towns, shipbuilding towns, fishing ports like Fleetwood and Grimsby, and in a sense specialized commercial towns like Manchester and Leeds. In addition there were the refuge towns for retired people, seaside and health resorts, and tourist centres. Even the old university towns of Oxford and Cambridge fitted comfortably into the new system of specialization. However, there continued to exist various mixed types of towns, particularly the non-specialized middle- and higher-rank traditional central places like the old county towns and commercial centres, at least those fortunate enough to be on one or more railway main lines so as to attract new industries or continue old ones.

The geographical effect of transport improvements under *laissez-faire* conditions was further to increase the economic strength of towns in already favourable locations, or with other existing advantages, so that particular towns experienced enormous growth. Correspondingly, towns without such advantages languished, especially many of the historically important county towns and countless small market towns. Among the rapidily growing towns, Manchester, Leeds, and Birmingham represented new commercial centres, Glasgow, Liverpool, Bristol, and Hull were major ports, and Aberdeen prospered as a specialized port. Lesser but still appreciable growth was experienced by old central places such as Norwich, York, Newcastle (Fig. 1), and Leicester. However, the most favoured cities in every respect were the two capital cities of Edinburgh and London (Fig. 2).[8]

Sometimes accelerated growth affected entire groups of towns, particularly in the coalfields and along the great tidal estuaries, where strings of towns coalesced to form conurbations. Even away from the main transport nodes popular and retirement towns could augment their size considerably in a short period (Fig. 3).

The same dogma of *laissez-faire* also dominated the mechanism of internal changes and the spatial expansion of towns. The primacy of private economic interests ruled everywhere as did the aversion to any form of public control. The power of such ideology accounts for the rapidity with which inner-city slums appeared,[9] and the piecemeal manner in which land and building speculation pushed the fringe of the urban tract outwards, stimulating activity just beyond the outskirts of the town where the financial climate for speculation was most favourable.

General aspects of the Victorian townscape[10]

These broad economic and social conditions were expressed in varying ways in the British townscape.[11] Different functional types of towns produced different townscapes. Most easily recognizable are those of single function towns developing either from nothing or from smaller settlements. Here the differences are indicated by the mine, iron foundry, steel mill, shipyard, cotton mill, or the great

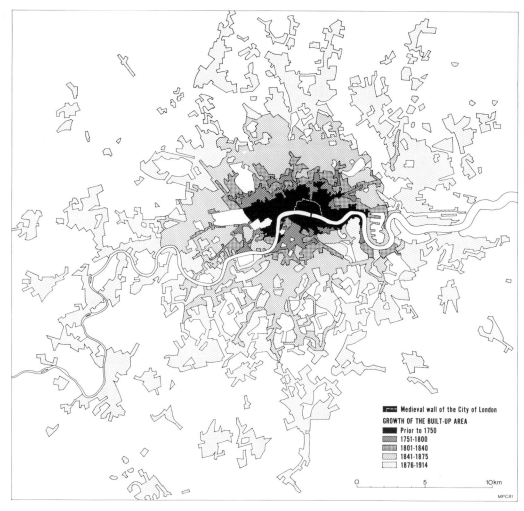

Figure 2. Growth of the built-up area of Greater London, 1750–1914. Based on various cartographic sources.

hotels, pump rooms or casinos, whereas the much larger associated residential areas exhibit considerable similarity from town to town.

In the majority of Victorian cities, however, the most important morphological contrast that developed was that between the urban core, on the one hand, and the peripheral accretionary integuments, increasingly more extensive, on the other.

Urban core and accretionary integuments

Strong morphological differentiation in the urban core resulted from the development of business cores and administrative centres in those towns that grew rapidly to great size and prestige in the later nineteenth century. In cities like Manchester and Liverpool, Birmingham and Leeds, and on a more modest scale in specialized industrial towns like Middlesbrough and Crewe or spas like

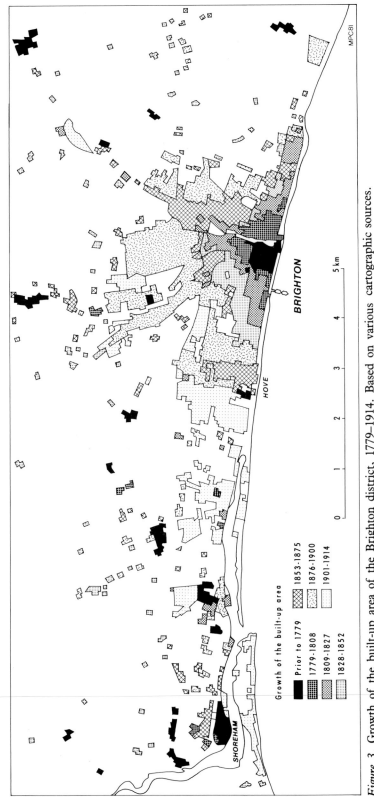

Growth of the built-up area

Prior to 1779   1853-1875
1779-1808   1876-1900
1809-1827   1901-1914
1828-1852

BRIGHTON

HOVE

SHOREHAM

0   1   2   3   4   5 km

MPC81

Figure 3. Growth of the built-up area of the Brighton district, 1779–1914. Based on various cartographic sources.

Cheltenham and Harrogate, the town centre was enriched through the appearance of new commercial and office buildings as well as public edifices of all kinds.

Even greater variety in urban forms arose in other towns from the presence of substantial traditional urban cores that were only slightly transformed during the era of industrialization. This applies particularly to those older and generally larger towns that were able to preserve and enhance their functional importance during this period and therefore experienced gradual transformative change of their traditional cores as well as additive outward growth on their peripheries. The higher the rank of the town as a central place the greater the inner differentiation of its business district, the variety of morphological processes involved enhancing the diversity in form content. This was particularly true in old regional centres like Norwich, York, Newcastle, Bristol, and Edinburgh, and above all in London.

The surrounding accretionary integuments contrast with the urban cores. Initially following the arterial roads, they form ultimately more or less concentric zones, though modified in various ways. These can be divided functionally, genetically, and morphologically into two kinds, namely residential accretions and, intercalated with these, urban fringe belts. The genetic significance of these two kinds will be discussed later.

Morphological periods

Further morphological differences came with changes in individual form elements in the course of townscape development. They arose in response to changes in the functional requirements of society, for example, those associated with the increasing division of labour and changes in living styles and cultural recreational activities. Since these facets of urban life did not develop independently of each other but rather as parts of a coherent socio-cultural system, each phase of this development has its distinctive overall character. This is reflected in the development of forms in the townscape and extends over the whole range of form categories (town plan, building fabric, and land and building utilization), thus leading to the recognition of distinctive morphological periods. These are the outcome of a wide variety of factors, including transport technology, public health and building legislation and residential architecture. The timing of the spread of innovations relating to each of these factors varies regionally, making it difficult to establish a chronologically identical period scheme over the whole country. However, a scheme that is valid in social and cultural terms can be devised on the basis of the architectural development of British urban house types and their associated types of town-plan units, the emphasis being on the socially significant spatial structure of the dwelling-house rather than its architectural style in the more restricted academic sense. Other urban building types as well as types of land and building utilization can without difficulty find their place within this period scheme. On this basis five periods can be distinguished: late-Georgian and Regency, early-Victorian, mid-Victorian, late-Victorian, and Edwardian.

The period of late-Georgian and Regency houses, from about 1760 to 1840, coincides with the first major growth phase of industrialization, and includes the eras of canal and turnpike building, and the first railway boom. During this period the first filling in or repletion of medieval burgages with small workers' houses occurred in the old towns, while arterial roads on the outskirts of towns became lined with modest middle-class housing, and great estates for the wealthy developed in London's West End.

In the early-Victorian period, from 1840 to about 1860, repletion of the old towns with working-class housing and industries continued and often reached saturation level, accompanied by notorious cholera epidemics. This period also covers the first great extension of the main-line railway network (the second railway boom) and considerable expansion of operational railway land around main-line stations inside big cities, above all in London. To this internal upheaval were added the first few cases of central commercial redevelopment by "break-through" streets. At the urban fringe, the first significant suburban extensions appeared on a broader front, consisting mainly of residential areas for the middle classes and upper working classes.

The mid-Victorian period, 1860 to 1875, was associated with continued railway building, further growth of slums, more break-through streets and considerable expansion of the built-up area, but still without really effective building control. Together, the early- and mid-Victorian periods coincided with the second phase of industrialization, a phase of expansion and maturation.

The late-Victorian period, from 1875 to 1895, coincides roughly with the so-called "Great Depression". All the previous processes intensified during this period, but to this were now added morphologically important innovations calculated to deal with the most pressing problems of urban development in the light of past experience. They were the introduction of public sanitary building control and related public utilities, and the first, albeit insufficient, attempts to cope with the slums and the need for working-class housing in inner-city areas. The characteristic morphological traits of this period resulted from the con-solidating Public Health Act of 1875. In addition, the commuting of workers in London and other large cities was improved by the Cheap Trains Act of 1883 and the provision of tramways and omnibuses. Finally, there was an acceleration in the growth of the co-operative housing associations for the provision of relatively inexpensive dwellings that had already appeared in the previous period.

The Edwardian period, from 1895 to 1914, coincided roughly with the last phase of economic development before the First World War, when the country's real national income ceased to grow for the first time for many years. While the building of railways came to an end, most of the other morphological processes mentioned earlier continued vigorously, together with new reforms in housing and town planning under the influence of the garden city movement.

Types of town plans and building types

This sequence of periods has found expression in the historical layering of the townscape, namely in the town plan and building fabric.[12] The plan types of the Georgian and Regency periods generally followed the principles of English classicism, distinguished by bold outlines and simplicity of design. This is well illustrated in the West End of London with its street systems that were simple yet always designed as a composition, punctuated here and there by the large rectangular "London Squares" with their tall trees (Fig 4).[13]

A good deal of this refined and confident expression of a high level of residential culture (Fig. 5) was carried over into the early-Victorian period in the subsequent development of upper- and middle-class areas. However, speculative pressures for increasingly rapid building development, associated with smaller plots and houses, soon lowered the general quality of residential areas. In the case of the smallest dwellings, intended for the lowest income groups and built without any pretence to architectural expression, all claims to what is humanly acceptable soon became lost under the pressure of a steeply rising demand for small dwellings, depressing even the standards of the first few reform attempts.[14] Especially in the booming towns of the industrial Midlands and northern England, this led to the construction of the notorious, ill-ventilated back-to-back houses, let by the week or even the day. Arranged mostly in double terraces, they reached residential densities of up to 150 dwellings per hectare (Fig. 6).[15] Intended theoretically as two- or three-room single-family houses, this type of housing frequently sheltered far greater numbers of people through illegal sub-letting as "lodging-houses", particularly in the great ports. Individual rooms, virtually devoid of furniture, often sheltered up to eight or ten persons of both sexes and all ages in a space of 10 square metres. The double terraces of back-to-backs, frequently grouped about inner courtyards, were either set within and adapted to the shape of already existing field or street blocks, or were mechanically arranged in new regular street grids. Such housing tracts, together with the type discussed next, were the worst breeding grounds of the cholera epidemics of the 1840s.[16] In towns with medieval centres, the historical predecessors of the back-to-back houses were the similar blind-back or half-back houses, squeezed as single rows against the side boundaries of an old strip plot or burgage, which are discussed later.[17] In addition there were the so-called through-houses (Fig. 7), built mainly in the mid-Victorian period for lower paid workers, which, though still small, did permit through ventilation. These houses were built in tight rows and before long, by virtue of their massive repetition, soon formed a dominant feature in many English industrial towns.[18]

Following the Public Health Act of 1875 and the beginning of the late-Victorian period, a new, improved terrace house type emerged (Fig. 8). It was based on the sanitary provisions of the new act and the corresponding local bye-laws, leading thus to widespread standardization. Each dwelling in the terrace had a small back wing jutting out at the rear to accommodate scullery and/or other utility rooms on

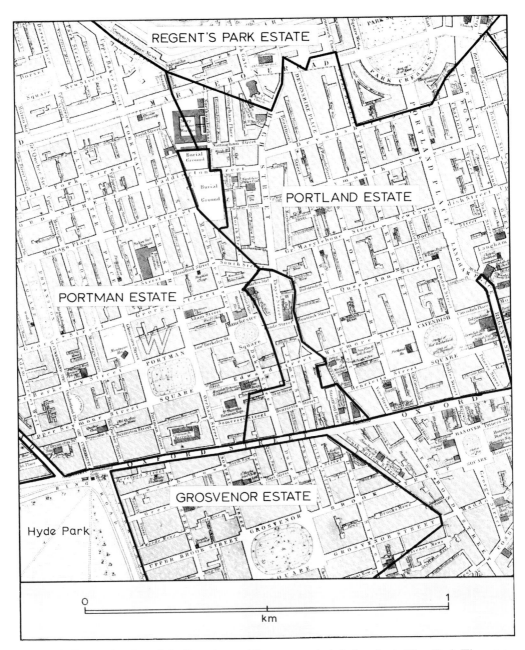

Figure 4. Estate planning of the Georgian and Regency periods in London's West End. The estate boundaries are based on Summerson, J. (1945) *Georgian London* (London) p. 149. The base map is reproduced from *The Weekly Dispatch Atlas*, 1857.

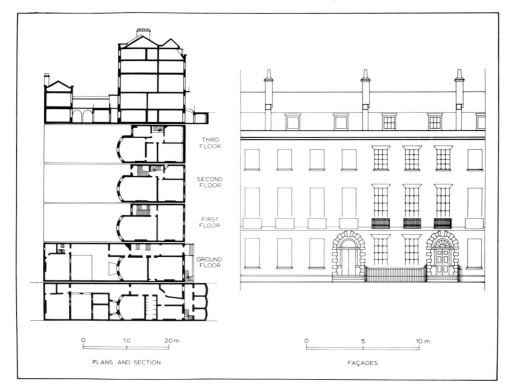

Figure 5. Georgian house in Bedford Square, Bloomsbury, London. Based on Rasmussen, S. E. (1960) *London: the unique city* (Harmondsworth) pp. 185–6.

the ground floor, often with an extra bedroom above. The repetition of this feature gave the terraces the serrated backsides which formed the salient characteristic of their block-plans. The new statutory requirement for separate front and back entrances for each house created the problem of access from the street to the rear of the terraces. In the West Midlands this was solved through tunnel-like connections on the ground floor of each terrace; therefore this house type is referred to in the literature, not very felicitously, as the "tunnel-back house".[19] Elsewhere, solutions often differed, mainly through the introduction of a back alley that served all houses simultaneously, so that the house type is probably better referred to as a back-wing house. It gained wide acceptance as the standard for speculative housing in various sizes and by no means only in the form of terraces. Thus, it was deemed suitable not only for working-class families but also for much of the middle class throughout southern England and as far north as Yorkshire and Cumberland, with residential densities of 50–75 dwellings per hectare. It was rendered obsolete only by the building legislation after the First World War. In the roughly 40 years of its existence this house type, together with the associated grids of "bye-law streets" contributed more than any other single form to the general character of the Victorian townscape. In north-east England a

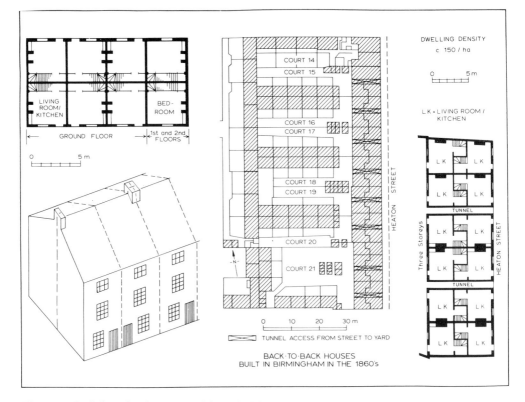

Figure 6. Building development with early-Victorian back-to-back houses. Based on Conzen, M. R. G. (1952) *Geographie und Landesplanung in England* Colloquium Geographicum 2 (Bonn) map 4, and Chapman, S. D. and Bartlett, J. N. (1971) "The contribution of building clubs and freehold land society to working-class housing in Birmingham", in Chapman, S. D. (ed.) *The history of working-class housing* (London) p. 229.

regional variant emerged in the back-wing flats in which each house contained two dwellings, one on each floor (Fig. 9).

Further north in Scotland, where the large cities were growing equally rapidly, the multi-storey, multi-family tenement, reminiscent of the continental *Miets-haus*, continued to dominate. With origins reaching far back into the pre-industrial period, this type assumed late-Georgian and then Victorian speculative forms (Fig. 10).[20] In England this tenement form was not common until the Edwardian period, and even then occurred in smaller numbers than in Scotland. Its two sharply contrasting types were the simple tenement building containing small flats to alleviate the demand for workers' housing in the inner areas of several large cities,[21] and the high-class luxury flats for the well-to-do in London's West End.

In general, however, wealthier townspeople of the Victorian and Edwardian periods followed the example of some of their late-Georgian predecessors in living on spacious park-adorned plots near the urban fringe in large, semi-detached, or more often detached, houses or villas. Such buildings had an unrestricted, often

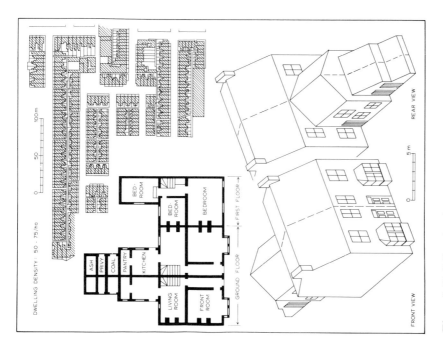

Figure 8. Building development with late-Victorian back-wing houses. Based on Conzen, M. R. G. (1952) *Geographie und Landesplanung in England* Colloquium Geographicum 2 (Bonn) map 4.

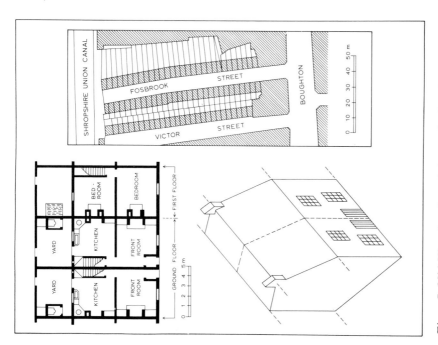

Figure 7. Mid-Victorian through-houses in the railway station and canal district of Chester. Based on Conzen, M. R. G. (1952) *Geographie und Landesplanung in England* Colloquium Geographicum 2 (Bonn) map 4, and Ordnance Survey 1/2500 plan (Cheshire Sheet 38.11, Edition of 1911).

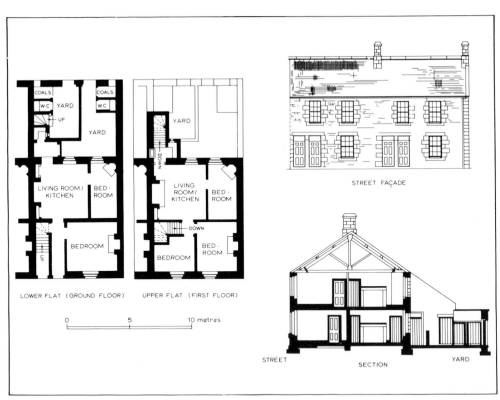

Figure 9. Northeast England back-wing flats of the late-Victorian and Edwardian period, Waggonway Road, Alnwick, Northumberland. Based on a building plan of 1897.

complicated plan with considerable internal corridor space and decorative façades expressive of particular style periods, especially after the industrial age finally abandoned English classicism in the 1860s in favour of architectural eclecticism (Fig. 11).

There is a rich technical literature of architectural pattern books and practical builders' manuals devoted to "desirable" Victorian and Edwardian residential house types and meant for owners as well as speculative builders. Subjects range from the large villa with at least ten rooms, excluding service quarters, to the smallest villa and working-man's cottage, treated with full attention to plans, elevations, historic styles used, and so forth.[22]

Finally, the reforms propagated by the garden city movement towards the end of the Edwardian period introduced more modern forms of semi-detached and detached houses of a size increasingly within the reach of middle-income groups (Fig. 12).[23] They occupied residential areas of more informal, open planning in deliberate rejection of the mechanical street grids of Victorian times. Residential densities averaged less than 20 dwellings per hectare and allowed the houses to appear embedded in their own gardens.

It is not possible here to consider the multiplicity of other urban building types. However, it is worth emphasizing the extraordinarily varied contribution made by

Figure 10. Tenements in Glasgow. Façades based on a photograph by T. R. Annan; plans based on Kellett, J. R. (1967) *Glasgow: a concise history* (London) p. 59.

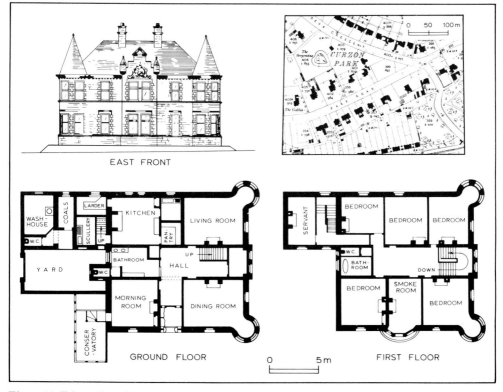

Figure 11. Edwardian villa in the French renaissance style and part of an Edwardian villa district in Chester. Based on a building plan of 1897 and the Ordnance Survey 1/2500 plan (Cheshire Sheet 38.15, Edition of 1911).

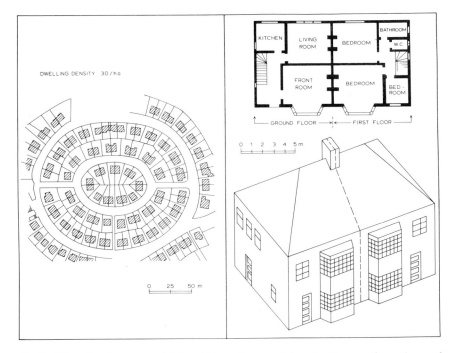

Figure 12. Building development with late-Edwardian semi-detached houses from the garden city movement.

the industrial era to the form enrichment of the urban cores of British towns, with hotels and boarding houses, churches, town halls, public buildings of all sorts, shops and office buildings, and specialized buildings for trade and industry. Virtually every town in the country is affected by this diversification, no matter how large or small it is.

Morphological processes in general

If the dynamics of the British townscape during the industrial era are to be understood, it is necessary to comprehend the individual forms and their spatial association today as the result of the various processes of townscape formation. Attention will be confined to some principal processes that affected British towns in general and are therefore of fundamental importance.[24]

As the majority of towns already existed when industrialization began in Britain, two principal groups of morphological processes have to be distinguished. Within already existing townscapes industrialization caused changes through transformative processes. In the course of time these affected nearly all existing towns, even the smallest, but differed greatly in the kind and intensity of their effects depending on the size, functional significance, and other circumstances of individual places. Beyond the limits of the pre-industrial townscape in old towns, and of course in all newly created urban settlements, the industrial era created entirely new forms, most notably a sequence of peripheral accretions.

Both groups of processes were controlled by basic socio-economic factors operating through the medium of land and building utilization. Morphological change in response to changing functional requirements tended to be abrupt in a short-term view focussed on local detail but continual in long-term perspective taking the townscape as a whole. It occurred generally in phases, from the occupation of unaltered existing forms, to their modification, and eventually to their replacement by more suitable new forms. We have here a cycle of reaction between form and function, such as is suggested in simpler terms by Neef's concept of "psychic ascent" (*psychische Treppe*).[25] Sooner or later new forms themselves succumb to this cycle in the tension between dynamic function and static form. The whole process can be conceived as a sequence of morphological tension cycles, each capable of repetition and/or variation.

In societies characterized by the primacy of unbridled economic purposes, as in the case of Britain during the industrial era, such development is liable to lead to the ruthless removal of inherited forms, destroying a society's sense of human continuity in its habitat. However, this is by no means inevitable if a society is orientated towards the totality of life, including its cultural and spiritual quality, without neglecting its economic requirements. Notable, if isolated, efforts in that direction were already evident in Britain towards the close of the industrial era, as exemplified by the Edwardian reconstruction of the famous medieval "Rows" in the Old Town of Chester.[26]

Throughout Britain the forces behind transformative and additive processes operated within the pre-existing cultural landscape which acted as a morphological frame and posed a physical as well as a spiritual challenge. In general the response in the landscape was an adaptation in varying degree, so that inherited traits, especially details of plan, shone through to endow the new townscape with the quality of historical layering. However, town plan, building fabric, and land and building utilization differed in the degree of resistance they offered to the pressure of functional demands. Land and building utilization proved to be least resistant to change, and the town plan most resistant. This complicates the historical layering of the townscape. Only very large capital expenditure could lead to the complete removal of the morphological frame, as in the case of railway construction in or close to town centres or the creation of break-through streets.

Transformative processes

The most important transformative processes in the cores of old towns are, first, building repletion, the gradual filling up of the existing townscape with additional buildings, and secondly, replacement of old forms by new ones, which can affect buildings, plots, streets, and land utilization singly or in combination in a variety of ways.

Building repletion

Building cheap lodgings for the rapidly growing working population contributed most to the building repletion of inner town quarters in the early stages of industrialization. Residence close to their places of work was essential for these workers because of the central locations of many industries at the time, the long working hours, insecure conditions of employment, extremely low wages, and lack of cheap public transport. These lowest income groups therefore put great pressure on space in the inner town, which was soon exploited in a brutal way by speculative construction of appalling dwellings on tiny patches of ground.

Repletion took a particular form in rapidly growing towns with medieval cores, especially if these were relatively small, as in Leeds, Liverpool, Manchester, and Birmingham, or where ancient urban plots or "burgages" of the north-west European shape (that is, narrow and very long) dominated the early plan, as in most of northern Britain. On these burgages building repletion soon went through the repletive and saturation or climax phases of the burgage cycle,[27] transforming the land behind the houses forming the street fronts into a dangerous, rat-infested slum. Its evils were aggravated by simultaneous colonization of these back yards with small industries of all kinds, pigsties, open refuse heaps, privies, and the like. With few exceptions the climax phase of the burgage cycle lasted from the 1840s or 1860s well into the Edwardian period, that is to say at least until the advent of the Housing of the Working Classes Acts of the 1890s and in some cases up to the First World War. The characteristic house type involved was the blind-back house which, in rows of up to 20 dwellings, transformed the former back gardens of the burgages into "courts" or "yards".

An example can be drawn from the market town of Alnwick in Northumberland to illustrate a widespread phenomenon. In the burgage of Teasdale's Yard, well documented[28] owing to its 17 cases of cholera in 1849 (five of them fatal), one can follow the progress of the burgage cycle through its institutive, repletive, climax, and recessive phases in the development of building coverage (i.e. the percentage of ground covered by buildings, calculated from large-scale town plans). In this case, the building coverage index stood at 14·7 per cent in 1774, 34·8 per cent in 1827, 62·9 per cent in 1849, 65·2 per cent in 1864, 65·2 per cent in 1921, and 19·3 per cent in 1956 (Fig. 13).[29]

The map for 1849 shows the building use at that date. Clearly, the blind-back houses, marked "TE", are intermixed with workshops, including a smithy, as well as pigsties, manure and refuse heaps, privies, and a "school" for beggar children. The whole group of buildings was demolished only in 1937 as part of a larger slum clearance scheme, after standing derelict and dilapidated for many years. Elsewhere in Alnwick such blind-back houses survived until recently. The burgage cycle just described is applicable to most parts of the small urban core of Alnwick with its more than one hundred burgages (Figs 14 and 15), and is a good example of the persistent influence exerted by an old morphological frame during a continuous process involving only minimal capital investment. Similar

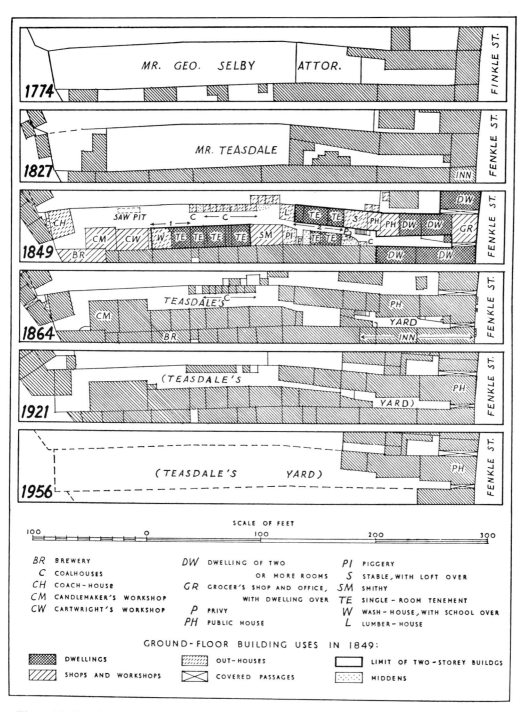

Figure 13. Teasdale's Yard, Fenkle Street, Alnwick, and its burgage cycle from 1774 to 1956. Reproduced from Conzen, M. R. G. (1960) *Alnwick, Northumberland: a study in town-plan analysis* Inst. Br. Geogr. Publ. No. 27, p. 68.

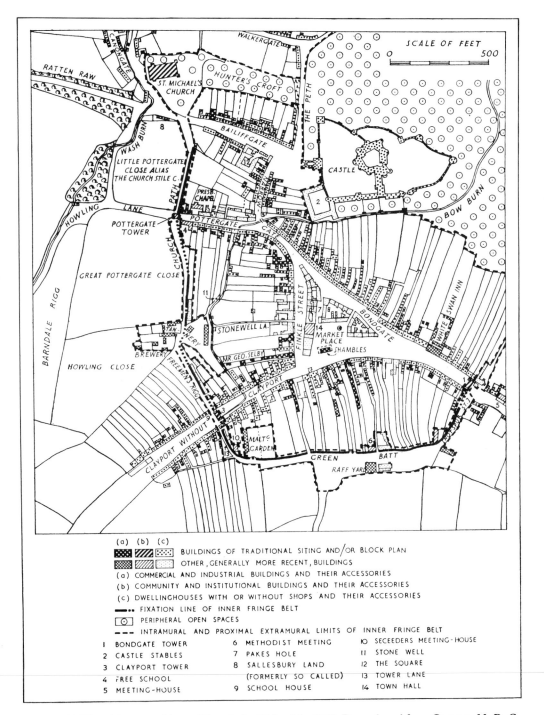

Figure 14. The old town and inner fringe belt of Alnwick, 1774. Reproduced from Conzen, M. R. G. (1960) *Alnwick, Northumberland: a study in town-plan analysis* Inst. Br. Geogr. Publ. No. 27, p. 57.

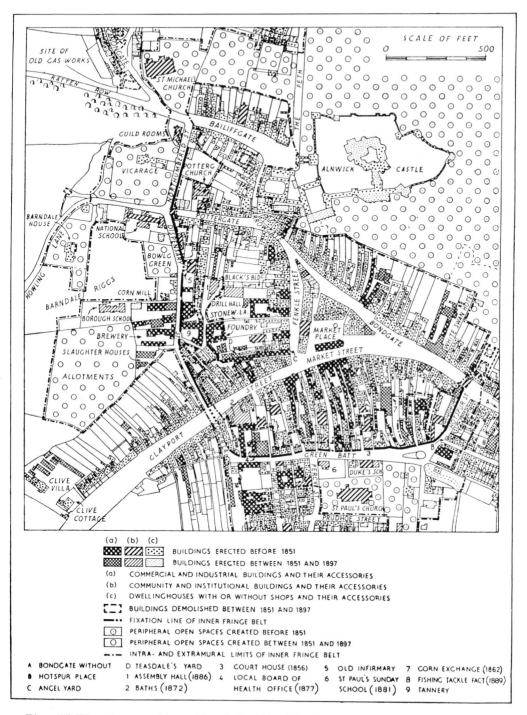

Figure 15. The old town and inner fringe belt of Alnwick, 1897. Reproduced from Conzen, M. R. G. (1960) *Alnwick, Northumberland: a study in town-plan analysis* Inst. Br. Geogr. Publ. No. 27, p. 76.

phenomena exist in large cities, though in more intensive form and sometimes associated with changes of function, as has been shown for burgage series in Newcastle.[30]

The replacement of old forms by new ones

The replacement of existing forms by new ones in old town centres, representing a morphological adaptation to the growth of business activities, involved two main types of processes, distinguished partly by their relative extent. In the case of small-scale, piecemeal replacement, individual buildings or small groups of buildings on the street front were replaced by more modern building types, often accompanied by the amalgamation of adjacent plots. Of course, this type of change had been known long before the industrial era, but it now acquired rather more significance through its great aggregate amount during the unprecedented intensification and expansion of the business core, especially in larger towns, and the associated spatial segregation of new specialized functions. As a piecemeal process it effaced the morphological frame at least partially and in the centres of large cities led frequently to considerable plot pattern metamorphosis (Fig. 16).[31]

More significant was the other kind of change in urban cores, namely central commercial redevelopment, consisting of the redevelopment of a larger tract of land according to a unified plan. Depending upon whether these schemes were adapted to a pre-existing street system or whether they involved the construction of new streets augmenting the system, one can speak of adaptive or augmentative redevelopment.[32] More important, however, is the functional purpose behind the redevelopment, not only because it determined the form but also because it could have drastic social consequences.[33] One such functionally defined type of re-

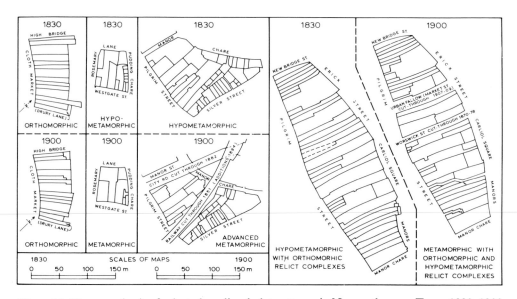

Figure 16. Metamorphosis of selected medieval plot patterns in Newcastle upon Tyne, 1830–1900.

development was the break-through street, designed as a traffic improvement, which was frequently employed in the large older cities during the industrial era, especially in London. In Newcastle it was used seven times between 1784 and 1882. Twice, in fact, break-through streets were instituted in conjunction with two more important functional types of redevelopment: one was the large-scale and skilfully designed comprehensive commercial redevelopment of an extensive business district with a system of no less than eight new streets in the centre of the Old Town in 1839; the other was the central railway viaduct constructions of 1849–51 (Fig. 17).[34]

These three functional types of redevelopment were widely used in British towns during the industrial era. They required considerable capital investment, effacement of the morphological frame and usually caused great dislocation of the land-use pattern of the affected areas. This is particularly true for the periods of major railway building in the nineteenth century, even in London where the railway companies seldom attempted to locate their great terminal stations any

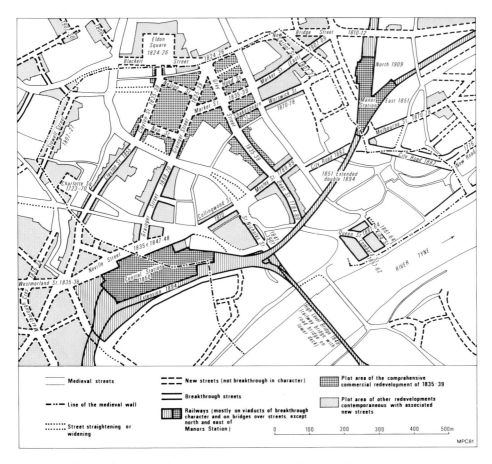

Figure 17. Redevelopment schemes in central Newcastle upon Tyne, 1784–1909.

RIVER IRWELL

0   1   2   3km

Urban fringes & urban fringe belts

—   Urban fringe of Manchester M & Salford S c. 1650

---   Urban fringe c. 1750

–·–   Urban fringe c. 1800

—   Outer limit of the urban fringe belt c. 1800

---   Outer limit of the urban fringe belt c. 1825

⊏⊐   Urban fringe belt elements from the period 1826-1855

⊏⊐   Urban fringe belt elements from the period 1856-1875

▭   Urban fringe belt elements from the period 1876-1900

Functional structure, circa 1900

▦   Central commercial district (offices, shops, larger public services, centrally located warehouses specializing in the cotton trade, etc.)

▥   Industrial areas (all types) and utility services

▧   Transport services, including all operational and storage areas (railways, canals, harbours, docks)

▨   Larger public and private institutions in original urban fringe belt location (hospitals, almshouses, prison, etc.)

▭   Recreational and other open spaces in original urban fringe belt location (parks, cemeteries, sports grounds, reservoirs)

Residential districts

▦   Slum districts, in part intermixed with industry

▦   Working class districts, built under older building bye-laws

▦   Working class and lower middle class districts, built under post-1875 building bye-laws

▭   Residential districts of middle (and some upper) classes, with larger terrace semi-detached and detached houses

Figure 18. The morphological and functional structure of Manchester and Salford in 1900. Note in particular the following: 1) the transformation of the old town of Manchester into the modern business core expanding to the south and west for 250 years, and also the transformation of Salford's old town into part of the inner industrial belt; 2) the relatively well-defined inner fringe belts of 1800 and 1825, with the industrial belt chiefly within and the great slum belt chiefly beyond the urban fringe of 1825; 3) the far more disjointed character of the fringe belts of 1856–75 and 1876–1900, with occasional outliers such as industries, transport facilities, public and private institutions, and recreational areas; 4) the segregation of residential districts by income classes, the general concentric zonation of which is considerably modified in detail by lines of transport, desirable residential sites (healthy high ground in the north-northwest, rural tranquility of the Mersey plain in the south) and other factors.

farther in than the nearest arterial and ring roads close to the urban fringe of the time.

Central redevelopment, however, displaced not only small industries of all kinds but above all the central slum districts with their very high densities of population, the removal of which became an important auxiliary purpose of the operation despite the total absence of provisions for rehousing the affected population.[35] The large numbers of displaced people of necessity had to find new shelter nearby and poured into and immediately beyond the adjacent zone of mixed industry, warehouses, and workers' dwellings that had developed just outside the former urban fringe. This created the notorious slum belt around the core of so many British cities during the industrial era. Repeated commercial redevelopment in conjunction with the increasing functional intensification of the business core eventually displaced the early innermost slums completely. Thus the new slum belt came during the Edwardian period to present the most important and acute housing problem in British cities all over the country. It could be found in Manchester (Fig. 18)[36] as much as in Birmingham, Glasgow or London and was so massive that it cast its shadow well into the inter-war period, in a number of cases even into the post-war period.

Additive processes

In turning to additive processes attention shifts from the realm of inner urban areas to that of the peripheral integuments. During the industrial era the outward expansion of British towns generally followed the major arterial roads at first, producing a tendency towards a star-shaped outline, though this was anything but regular. Most of the population, however, could not consider long journeys to work since only the well-to-do could afford the necessary means of transport.

London at that time was an exception, since there the railway companies, even before the Cheap Trains Act of 1883, had discovered a lucrative source of income in cheap workmen's tickets, which contributed substantially to the enormous areal growth of the capital (Fig. 2).[37] As the imperial metropolis, London is altogether a special case, its suburban expansion beginning much earlier than elsewhere.[38]

In the larger towns, where industry was normally located in and around the inner slum belt, a combination of concentric and radial growth was usual, the actual shape of the built-up area depending on factors such as topography or the contingencies of access by speculative builders to new building land. In the case of specialized towns like the cotton towns of south-east Lancashire, growth was governed largely by the more scattered arrangement of the textile mills, the workers being housed in close proximity to these. In the big cities with mixed industrial and commercial functions, however, the built-up area expanded somewhat more regularly around the inner city and its slum belt.

Urban growth did not proceed steadily as it depended on fluctuations in the economy, building cycles[39] and other factors. The urban fringe accelerated or decelerated its outward advance accordingly and could come to a temporary halt during a housebuilding slump. In such a case a motley group of urban land uses normally seeking spacious and cheaper sites at the periphery tended to fill in the belt of open land immediately outside the stationary urban fringe as typical fringe-belt elements, the more so as some were subject to their own cycles of development with phasing different from, and occasionally even opposed to, that of the housebuilding cycle. Once started this development could gradually preclude further housebuilding in the belt, even if a later housebuilding boom caused the urban fringe to continue its outward advance.[40] The process was repeated several times especially in larger towns, depending on regional variations in the timing of the building cycle. Eventually this led to a rough, sometimes weakly developed, concentric arrangement of functionally contrasted urban integuments in which predominantly residential accretions of varying width alternated with urban fringe belts of mixed, initially peripheral, land uses.[41] The whole arrangement is analogous to the annual growth rings of a tree trunk (Fig. 18).

In general the new forms created by the growth processes of the industrial era were adapted more or less to the pre-existing morphological frame, without destroying it. Thus most of the old roads and settlement nuclei survived in the expanding built-up area and so did many of the field boundaries as ownership boundaries in various forms. However, residential accretions and urban fringe belts show certain differences in their relationship to the morphological frame.

The formation of residential accretions

Residential accretions comprise the most striking spatial component of the Victorian suburbs and in their massive appearance anticipate the collective term "suburbia"—a somewhat derisive term first used for the urban expansion of the inter-war period.

Amalgamation of fields occurred in cases of comprehensive building development by large landowners or builders, and later also building societies. More often, however, the inherited irregular field pattern was adhered to in new building development because of the organizational scale predominant in the Victorian and Edwardian periods.[42] While there were both large and small building firms, reflected to some extent in the large variations in the size of individual building estates, it was the small builders that were by far the most numerous. Operating speculatively on limited credit they were able to proceed only with relatively small building schemes, erecting single-family dwellings in the form of "bye-law" terraces for a range of income classes. As a result, building operations advanced field by field, in comparatively small estates aggregated in a cellular or mosaic pattern with access through single residential streets or limited grids independent of one another. Often these were poorly connected, if at all, the links across old field boundaries tending to be in an awkward, crooked fashion (Fig. 19). This pattern of discordant development was typical of the activity of

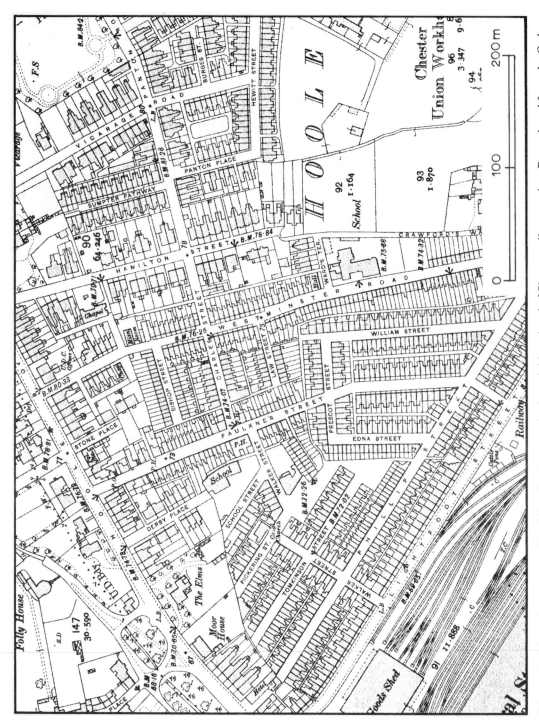

Figure 19. Discordant street and building development in the neighbourhood of Chester railway station. Reproduced from the Ordnance Survey 1/2500 plan (Cheshire Sheet 38.11, Edition of 1911).

small builders, particularly when they were involved in building small houses at high densities. Old field boundaries likewise often survived in the construction of villas because the average field size was sufficient, even with irregular outlines, to allow for the park-like layout of the grounds attached to each villa.

As a general rule spontaneous segregation of the income classes enabled the wealthy to live at or beyond the periphery in close contact with rural surroundings (Fig. 18). Frequently they preferred the socially more desirable west side of towns so that the "West End" and "East End" with their respective outer suburbs contrasted socially, as happened quite early in London. As the built-up area expanded outward there was a tendency for residential areas formerly on the fringe to lose social status as they became deeply embedded within the main body of the built-up area, resulting frequently in the subdivision of large plots and houses. This generalization does not apply, of course, in cases of special functional circumstances. In London during the late-Victorian period and increasingly during the Edwardian period, for example, large landowners and speculative investment companies put up expensive residential accommodation at exclusive addresses well inside the built-up area, especially in the old West End, to attract the upper classes. Another variant occurred in Oxford where professorial families, which at least up to the First World War belonged to the upper middle classes, created a large exclusive residential quarter in the sector-shaped "North Oxford" stretching from St Giles to the Victorian periphery.

Though the villas of the well-to-do occupied a portion of the urban area disproportionate to their numbers, the general character of urban residential areas was more strikingly determined by the areas occupied by the middle- and lower-income groups. The chief reason for this was the English tradition of single-family dwellings and its corollary, the provision of two- to three-storey terrace houses. Further, there was the advanced standardization and mass repetition of plot and house types, particularly those of the bye-law period after 1875, both in the working-class areas and those of the white collar employees and lower-middle classes. All this created the monotonous uniformity characteristic of the majority of Victorian suburbs. Only careful observation and comparative study of Victorian towns will reveal the subtle differences in the total stock of house types resulting from local factors, such as the different attitudes and responses of local authorities and builders to building legislation that was enabling rather than mandatory as regards implementation by local building bye-laws (Fig. 20).[43] Otherwise the residential monotony was interrupted but little by churches and schools and by the somewhat more varied forms of local shopping areas along the old highways and in former village nuclei. Nor was it relieved much by any diversifying effect of the morphological frame, such as the influence of old field boundaries on the grouping of forms.

Beyond these details of spatial grouping, however, Victorian residential areas displayed a much more marked segregation of functionally differentiated quarters by income classes than had been the case in the towns of pre-industrial times. To be sure, the result was by no means always a bold pattern of separation in large

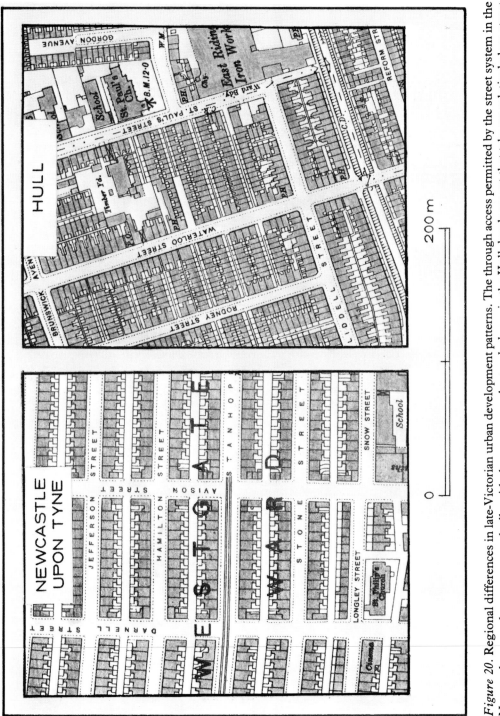

Figure 20. Regional differences in late-Victorian urban development patterns. The through access permitted by the street system in the Newcastle example contrasts markedly with the numerous short *culs-de-sac* in the Hull development that take up relatively less street space and are therefore more advantageous for the speculative builder. Reproduced from the Ordnance Survey 1/2500 plans (Northumberland Sheet 94.12, Edition of 1919, and Yorkshire (East Riding) Sheet 240.3, Edition of 1910).

tracts. Wealthy districts not only had their numerous domestic servants living in the houses of their employers but also an appreciable complementary population of working-class families providing a whole range of local services. This population lived in relatively close proximity on the backsides of the exclusive residential streets, usually in short streets of small terrace houses.

The formation of urban fringe belts

Urban fringe belts contrasted with residential accretions in their general plan structure as much as in their building types (Fig. 18). The diversity of land-use elements involved gave greater variety to the landscape. In addition, they exhibited considerably lower building densities in conjunction with a coarse-grained spatial structure, particularly in the case of the middle and outer fringe belts. This resulted from the common demand for large land parcels for such uses as cemeteries, sports grounds (especially golf courses), schools, and certain industries and utility services. Since such functions required few if any new streets, the existing morphological frame hardly required any change except for the occasional amalgamation of adjacent fields. In this way a free fringe belt, namely one still in direct contact with the surrounding countryside as distinct from an occluded fringe belt inside the built-up area, could for a long time, in parts at least, preserve the charm and peace of its rural origins. Large villas or even country seats fitted into such situations without difficulty, effecting easy transitions between residential accretions and fringe belts in the context of a more open landscape.

Land-use elements in fringe belts also tended to segregate in specialized functional sectors. Such sorting took place most clearly in the inner fringe belts of large cities, since here the proximity of a large and strongly diversified city centre engendered this transformation (Fig. 21). Thus the inner fringe belt experienced a characteristic, intensified development during the industrial era after a long pre-industrial and fairly stationary fixation phase. Its development in the industrial era consisted of two phases. The first was the expansion phase lasting from the mid-eighteenth to the mid-nineteenth century, that is before it had been hemmed in or occluded by significant growth beyond its outer limits. This phase contains the early stages of three morphological processes: first, increasing accumulation of diverse fringe-belt elements which enlarged the belt outwards and made it denser; secondly, incipient building repletion of certain fringe-belt elements because of intensified use; and thirdly, instances of site succession by different fringe-belt elements on the same plot, reflecting the progressive adaptation of the inner fringe belt to the increasing functional differentiation required by the urban core.

Then followed the consolidation phase, in which the inner fringe belt became increasingly occluded by the adjacent integument. Each of the three morphological processes just noted intensified to reach a mature stage. In addition functional segregation appeared as a new phenomenon to produce the functional sectors

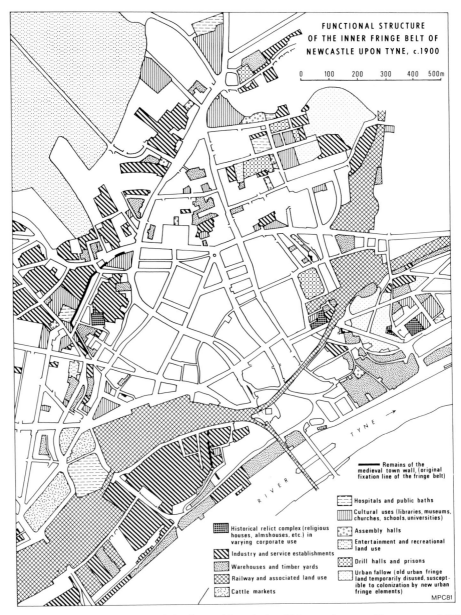

FUNCTIONAL STRUCTURE
OF THE INNER FRINGE BELT OF
NEWCASTLE UPON TYNE, c.1900

0   100   200   300   400 500m

━━ Remains of the
medieval town wall, (original
fixation line of the fringe belt)

Hospitals and public baths

Cultural uses (libraries, museums,
churches, schools, universities)

Assembly halls

Entertainment and recreational
land use

Drill halls and prisons

Urban fallow (old urban fringe
land temporarily disused, susceptible to colonization by new urban
fringe elements)

Historical relict complex (religious
houses, almshouses, etc.) in
varying corporate use

Industry and service establishments

Warehouses and timber yards

Railway and associated land use

Cattle markets

MPC81

Figure 21. Functional structure of the inner fringe belt of Newcastle upon Tyne around 1900.

already referred to. These sectors had their origin in the rising demand in late-Victorian and Edwardian city life for all kinds of central services, which sought proximity to the centre of the city. Thus new zones of functional specialization were formed in the inner fringe belt, either as more or less clearly defined institutional precincts, such as those for colleges, major hospitals, and certain cultural and administrative functions, or as even more extensive tracts devoted to technical or economic specialization, such as the railway, warehousing, and certain industries.[44]

Clearly, the processes operating in the inner fringe belt of a large city during the industrial era served to transform it increasingly into a functionally complementary space to the business core. In this way the belt lost completely that loose areal texture which in later fringe belts serves as a reminder of the original rural context. In fact, the old coarse grain and immaturity of its original street system was changed by the construction of new break-through streets, connecting streets, and local access streets.

Thus at the end of this transformation the townscape of the inner fringe belt resembled in some ways that of the adjacent areas of highest building density, namely, the business core and the slum belt. Nevertheless, after more than 150 years of site succession and many other changes, the distinctiveness of its land-use pattern, the peculiarities of its street system and the occasional relict forms were still extant as reminders of its original fringe character, preserving the functional as well as the historico-genetic unity of the inner fringe belt well beyond the Edwardian period.

The total character of the Victorian townscape

The most outstanding feature of the British townscape in the industrial era is the enormous extent of the Victorian and Edwardian integuments compared with those of earlier periods. Although the large majority of these areas were to be found in the conurbations and the large and medium-sized towns, there were comparatively few small towns that did not share at least minimally in this development.

Much of this urban expansion involved industrial and transport installations which sometimes lent special accent to the urban physiognomy, particularly to the fringe belts. The general impression throughout the country, however, was dominated by the residential tracts, especially the lower middle- and working-class areas that occurred in all towns. Their monotony, mentioned earlier, seemed to give all towns the same face.

Contrasting strongly with this monotony was the extreme diversity of forms in the city centres. It was intensified by the generally greater number of storeys and the incredible mixture of eclectic architectural styles that changed with architectural fashions, certain styles tending to become assigned to particular functional types of buildings. A certain order in this confusion of forms was achieved in larger towns by the increasing segregation of specialized functional zones in the town centre. During the mid- and late-Victorian period the same area acquired such large public buildings as town halls, assembly rooms, and museums, as special accents within the centre. However, the diffusion of architectural styles tended to take place on a national scale so that British town centres resembled each other to some degree, unless they were graced by a substantial stock of pre-industrial forms as was the case in many a county town.

On the whole then, urban development during the industrial era tended towards increasing uniformity of British townscapes and a weakening of their inherited individuality. Especially in the case of towns that grew to become the new large cities of the Victorian era, it is not always easy to recognize in their townscapes the socio-political individuality that Asa Briggs has described so vividly in his assessment of their municipal history.[45]

Other factors worked in the same direction. The great areal expansion and the considerable scale of the earth-moving activities of the period often effaced the topographical peculiarities of urban sites which had contributed considerably to the individuality of towns from the Middle Ages until the early nineteenth century. In addition, improvements in communications diffused new ideas and the new products of industrial mass production more rapidly. Together with the increasing national building legislation and the associated nation-wide spread of building standards, this contributed considerably to the effacement of the old regional variations in traditional house types and building materials. Finally, the accelerated functional development of the commercial cores stimulated high replacement rates of inherited forms in the historic centres, so that piecemeal destruction of the historic townscape also prejudiced the individuality of towns.

Thus the industrial era weakened the marked variety of historical townscapes in the country and replaced it partly by townscapes fashioned on a new economic principle of morphological variation through functional differentiation in the new hierarchy of central places, or through functional specialization, under conditions of nation-wide standardization of form detail. However, there was no large-scale destruction of traditional forms in the country as a whole because large numbers of old-established towns were comparatively unaffected by the pressures exerted by the new economic system and in a number of cases there was local resistance to large-scale change. Many medium-sized and small towns were able to retain their historical character, even though their business cores received many new building types. Moreover, a certain reaction against the destruction of historical townscapes set in towards the end of the period, leading increasingly to the stylistic assimilation of new buildings to the prevailing stock of forms in urban cores, as in the case of Chester noted earlier. By the end of the Edwardian period British townscapes as a whole still presented a rich and varied picture, composed of the old and the new, in spite of the force and scale with which the industrial era had established its own forms throughout the country.

Notes

1. Bobek, H. (1962) "Über den Einbau der sozialgeographischen Betrachtungsweise in die Kulturgeographie", *Deutscher Geographentag Köln 1961* (Wiesbaden) pp. 148–65, reprinted in Storkebaum, W. (ed.) (1969) *Sozialgeographie* (Darmstadt) pp. 75–103.

2. Schwind, M. (1951) "Kulturlandschaft als objektivierter Geist", *Dte geogr. Bl.* **46**, 5–28.

3. Martin, G. H. (1968) "The town as palimpsest", in Dyos, H. J. (ed.) *The study of urban history* (London) pp. 155–69.

4. Clapham, J. H. (1939–51) *Economic history of modern Britain* (Cambridge) 3 vols; Slater, G. (1932) *The growth of modern England* (London); Trevelyan, G. M. (1944) *English social history* (London) Chs 11–18; Smith, W. (1968) *An historical introduction to the economic geography of Great Britain* (London); Darby, H. C. (1973) (ed.) *A new historical geography of England* (Cambridge) Chs 7–12; Lawton, R. (1964) "Historical geography: the industrial revolution", in Watson, J. W. and Sissons, J. B. (eds) *The British Isles* (Edinburgh) pp. 221–44. For a historico-geographical summary see Conzen, M. R. G. (1952) *Geographie und Landesplanung in England* Colloquium Geographicum 2 (Bonn).

5. Royal Commission on Population (1949) *Report* Cmd 7695 (London); Law,C. M. (1967) "The growth of urban population in England and Wales, 1801–1911", *Trans. Inst. Br. Geogr.* **41**, 125–43; Lawton, R. (1968) "Population changes in England and Wales in the later nineteenth century", *Trans. Inst. Br. Geogr.* **44**, 55–74. On urban growth more generally see Weber, A. F. (1899) *The growth of cities in the nineteenth century: a study in statistics* (New York).

6. Owing to difficulties of interpretation with the English censuses of the nineteenth century, some of these figures remain controversial (cf. Law, op. cit. (note 5)) but this is not likely to affect the overall picture appreciably.

7. On urban growth in general, in addition to the literature cited in notes 4 and 5, see Lawton, R. (1972) "An age of great cities", *Tn Plann. Rev.* **43**, 199–224; Briggs, A. (1967–68) "The Victorian city: quantity and quality", *Vict. Stud.* **11**, 711–30; Best, G. (1967–68) "The Scottish Victorian city", *Vict. Stud.* **11**, 329–58.

8. Gomme, G. L. (1898) *London in the reign of Victoria* (London); Gomme, G. L. (1908) "London in the reign of Victoria", *Geogrl. J.* **30**, 489–509, 616–40; Shannon, H. A. (1935) "Migration and the growth of London", *Econ. Hist. Rev.* **5**, 79–86; Mayne, D. (1952) *The growth of London* (London); Royal Scottish Geographical Society (1919) "The early views and maps of Edinburgh 1544–1852", *Scott. geogr. Mag.* **35**, 281–329, which contains a map showing urban growth up to the First World War; Wise, M. J. and Thorpe, P. O'N. (1950) "The growth of Birmingham 1800–1950", in Kinvig, R. H., Smith, J. G. and Wise, M. J. (eds) *Birmingham and its regional setting* (Birmingham) pp. 213–28; Edwards, K. C. (1966) "The geographical development of Nottingham", in Edwards, K. C. (ed.) *Nottingham and its region* (Nottingham) pp. 363–404; Conzen, M. R. G. (1949) "Geographical setting of Newcastle", in Isaac, P. C. G. and Allan, R. E. A. (eds) *Scientific survey of north-eastern England* (Newcastle) pp. 191–7; Mitchell, J. B. (1965) "Cambridge: its origin and growth", in Steers, J. A. (ed.) *The Cambridge region* (Cambridge) pp. 162–78.

9. Dyos, H. J. (1967) "The slums of Victorian London", *Vict. Stud.* **11**, p. 34 ff.

10. For the development of the morphological concepts used here see Chapter 2 and Conzen, M. R. G. (1960) *Alnwick, Northumberland: a study in town-plan analysis* Inst. Br. Geogr. Publ. No. 27, reprinted 1969.

11. Betjeman, J. (1956) *The English town in the last hundred years* (London); Dyos, H. J. and Wolff, M. (eds) (1973) *The Victorian city: images and realities* (London) 2 vols; Briggs, A. (1963) *Victorian cities* (London).

12. Chapters 2 and 3. See also Conzen (1960) op. cit. (note 10); Conzen, M. R. G. (1958) "The growth and character of Whitby", in Daysh, G. H. J. (ed.) *A survey of Whitby and its surrounding area* (Eton) pp. 49–89, with two coloured folded maps at the scale of 1/2609.

13. Summerson, J. (1945) *Georgian London* (London); Rasmussen, S. E. (1960) *London: the unique city* (Harmondsworth).

14. Tarn, J. N. (1971) *Working-class housing in nineteenth-century Britain* (London);

Rimmer, W. G. (1961) "Working-men's cottages in Leeds, 1770–1840", *Thoresby Soc. Publs* **46**, 165–99.

15. See, for example, Beresford, M. W. (1971) "The back-to-back house in Leeds, 1787–1937", in Chapman, S. D. (ed.) *The history of working-class housing* (Newton Abbot) pp. 93–132; Chapman, S. D. (1971) "Working-class housing in Nottingham during the industrial revolution", in Chapman, op. cit. pp. 133–64; Chapman, S. D. and Bartlett, J. N. (1971) "The contribution of building clubs and freehold land society to working-class housing in Birmingham", in Chapman, op. cit. pp. 221–46; Bournville Village Trust (1941) *When we build again* (London) pp. 34–5; Chambers, J. D. (1945) *Modern Nottingham in the making* (Nottingham). Two examples from the voluminous earlier literature are Marr, T. R. (1904) *Housing conditions in Manchester and Salford* (Manchester) pp. 35–7, and Sayle, A. (1924) *The houses of the workers* (London) pp. 29–35, 37–40.

16. Creighton, C. (1894) *A history of epidemics in Britain* (London) 2 vols; Simon, J. (1887) *Public health reports* (London) 2 vols; Simon, J. (1890) *English sanitary institutions* (London).

17. Conzen (1960) op. cit. (note 10) retains the more general technical term "back-to-back house" for this special variant as is also the case in Beresford, op. cit. pp. 98–100, 108 (note 15), Chapman, op. cit. pp. 140, 198 (note 15), and Chapman and Bartlett, op. cit. pp. 224–5 (note 15).

18. Marr, op. cit. pp. 37–8 (note 15); Chapman and Bartlett, op. cit. p. 229 (note 15).

19. Sayle, op. cit. pp. 152–8 (note 15); Bournville Village Trust, op. cit. pp. 36–7 (note 15); Chapman and Bartlett, op. cit. pp. 232, 242 (note 15).

20. Butt, J. (1971) "Working-class housing in Glasgow, 1851–1914", in Chapman, S. D. (ed.) op. cit. pp. 55–92 (note 15).

21. Tarn, J. N. (1973) *Five per cent philanthropy: an account of housing in urban areas between 1840 and 1914* (Cambridge).

22. Loudon, J. C. (1836) *An encyclopaedia of cottage, farm and villa architecture and furniture* (London) 2 vols; Loudon, J. C. (1838) *Suburban architect and landscape gardener* (London); Brooks, S. H. (1839) *Designs for cottage and villa architecture* (London); Hole, J. (1866) *Homes of the working classes, with suggestions for their improvement* (London); Audsley, W. and G. (1868) *Cottage, lodge and villa architecture* (London); Richardson, C. J. (1870) *Picturesque designs for mansions, villas, lodges etc.* (London); Wilkes, C. (1897) *Handy book of villa architecture* (London); Dobson, E. (1849) *Rudiments of the art of building* (London); Simon, J. D. (1870) *The house-owner's estimator* (London). On Victorian "pattern books" see Harling, R. (1938) *Home: a Victorian Vignette* (London), and Dutton, R. (1954) *The Victorian home* (London). See also the elevations in Dyos, H. J. (1961) *Victorian suburb: a study of the growth of Camberwell* (Leicester) Ch. 7.

23. Howard, E. (1898) *Tomorrow* (London); Ashworth, W. (1954) *The genesis of modern British town planning* (London); Cherry, G. E. (1974) *The evolution of British town planning* (London).

24. On the principles and conceptualizations underlying the discussions in this and later sections see Chapter 2 and Conzen (1960) op. cit. (note 10).

25. Neef, E. (1951–52) *Das Kausalitätsproblem in der Entwicklung der Kulturlandschaft* Wissenschaftliche Zeitschrift der Universität Leipzig, Philosophisch-Historische Klasse 2, pp. 81–91; Neef, E. (1967) *Die theoretischen Grundlagen der Landschaftslehre* (Gotha) pp. 51–3.

26. Pevsner, N. (1971) *Cheshire* (Harmondsworth) pp. 132, 160–171; Insall, D. W. and associates (1968) *Chester: a study in conservation. Report to the Minister of Housing and*

Local Government and the City of Chester (London) pp. 23, 86–9, 112–29.

27. See Chapter 2 and Conzen (1960) op. cit. pp. 65–9, 77–80, 92–4 (note 10).

28. Rawlinson, R. (1850) *Report to the General Board of Health on a preliminary inquiry into the sewerage, drainage, and supply of water, and the sanitary conditions of the inhabitants of the township of Alnwick and Canongate in the County of Northumberland* (London).

29. Conzen (1960) op. cit. p. 92 (note 10).

30. Chapter 2, Figure 14.

31. Ibid. Figure 15.

32. Ibid. Figure 16.

33. Edwards, P. J. (1898) *London street improvements* (London); Dyos, H. J. (1957) "Urban transformation: the objects of street improvement in Regency and early Victorian London", *Int. Rev. Soc. Hist.* **2**, 259–65; Allan, C. M. (1965) "The genesis of British urban redevelopment with special reference to Glasgow", *Econ. Hist. Rev.* 2nd Ser. **18**, 598–613.

34. Wilkes, L. and Dodds, G. (1964) *Tyneside classical* (London); Middlebrook, S. (1950) *Newcastle upon Tyne: its growth and achievement* (Newcastle upon Tyne) Chs 14, 17, 20; Boyd, W. (1909) *Plan of Newcastle upon Tyne* (Newcastle upon Tyne)—this plan shows the streets, railways etc. of 1909 superimposed on the plan of 1830, with explanations.

35. Dyos, H. J. (1955) "Railways and housing in Victorian London", *J. Transp. Hist.* **2**, 11–21, 90–100; Dyos, H. J. (1957) "Counting the cost of railways", *Amat. Hist.* **4**, 191–7; Dyos, H. J. (1957–58) "Some social costs of railway building in London", *J. Transp. Hist.* **3**, 23–30; Kellett, J. R. (1969) *The impact of railways on Victorian cities* (London).

36. The coloured map of residential conditions in Manchester in 1904 at the scale of approximately 1/25 300 in Marr, op. cit. (note 15) illustrates a classical case. See also Chambers, op. cit. (note 15).

37. Sekon, G. A. (1938) *Locomotion in Victorian London* (London); Dyos, H. J. (1953–54) "Workmen's fares in south London, 1860–1914", *J. Transp. Hist.* **1**, 3–19.

38. Low, S. J. (1891) "The rise of the suburbs", *Contemp. Rev.* **60**, p. 547 ff; Dyos, H. J. (1954) "The growth of a pre-Victorian suburb: south London 1580–1836", *Tn Plann. Rev.* **25**, p. 67 ff. The best work is Dyos (1961) op. cit. (note 22). See also notes 8 and 13.

39. Lewis, J. P. (1965) *Building cycles and Britain's growth* (London); Cooney, E. W. (1960) "Long waves in building in the British economy of the nineteenth century", *Econ. Hist. Rev.* 2nd Ser. **13**, 257–69; Weber, B. (1955) "A new index of residential construction, 1938–1950", *Scott. J. Polit. Econ.* **2**, 104–32; Chalklin, C. W. (1974) *The provincial towns of Georgian England: a study of the building process 1740–1820* (London); Cairncross, A. K. and Weber, B. (1956) "Fluctuations in building in Great Britain, 1785–1849", *Econ. Hist. Rev.* 2nd Ser. **9**, 283–97; Shannon, H. A. (1934) "Bricks: a trade index, 1785–1849", *Economica* N.S. **1**, 300–18; Kenwood, A. G. (1963) "Residential building activity in north-eastern England, 1853–1913", *Manchr Sch.* **31**; Cooney, E. W. (1949) "Capital exports and investment in building in Britain and the United States, 1856–1914", *Economica* N.S. **16**, 347–54; Cairncross, A. K. (1953) *Home and foreign investment* (Cambridge); Saul, S. B. (1962) "English building fluctuations in the 1890s", *Econ. Hist. Rev.* 2nd Ser. **15**, 119–37.

40. See Chapter 2 and Conzen (1960) op. cit. pp. 56–65, 80–2, 105–7, 100, 114–15 (note 10). Other studies on this topic include Whitehand, J. W. R. (1967) "Fringe belts: a neglected aspect of urban geography", *Trans. Inst. Br. Geogr.* **41**, 223–33; Whitehand, J.

W. R. (1972a) "Building cycles and the spatial pattern of urban growth", *Trans. Inst. Br. Geogr.* **56**, 39–55; Whitehand, J. W. R. (1972b) "Urban-rent theory, time series and morphogenesis: an example of eclecticism in geographical research", *Area* **4**, 215–22; Whitehand, J. W. R. (1974) "The changing nature of the urban fringe: a time perspective", in Johnson, J. H. (ed.) *Suburban growth: geographical processes at the edge of the western city* (London) pp. 31–52; Barke, M. (1974) "The changing urban fringe of Falkirk: some morphological implications of urban growth", *Scott. geogr. Mag.* **90**, 85–97; Whitehand, J. W. R. (1975) "Building activity and intensity of development at the urban fringe: the case of a London suburb in the nineteenth century", *J. hist. Geogr.* **1**, 211–24.

41. The concept and term "urban fringe belt" (*Stadtrandzone*) originated in Louis, H. (1936) "Die geographische Gliederung von Gross-Berlin", *Länderkundliche Forschung Krebs-Festschrift*, 146–71.

42. See, for example, Hoskins, W. G. (1955) *The making of the English landscape* (London) p. 223, and above all Dyos (1961) op. cit. Chs 4 and 5 (note 22).

43. See, for example, Forster, C. A. (1972) "Court housing in Kingston upon Hull: an example of cyclic processes in the morphological development of nineteenth century bye-law housing", *Univ. of Hull Occ. Pap. Geogr.* **19**.

44. See Chapter 2.

45. Briggs, op. cit. (note 11).

SIX

Conzenian ideas: extension and development

J. W. R. WHITEHAND

Although the papers in this volume constitute a distinctive view of the urban landscape and not a comprehensive one, they stem from a broad perspective.[1] This may help to explain the varied directions that have been taken by those attempting to build on Conzen's work. Whereas an assessment of extensions of his research on town plans takes us into the local historical literature, tracing one of the lines of descent from perhaps the most fruitful of the concepts in this research takes us to the periphery of neo-classical economics.[2] But this variety of intellectual progeny is not matched by the language areas over which Conzen's influence has extended. Those taking up his ideas have been almost entirely confined to the English-speaking world; at first sight a remarkable fact in the light of the central European antecedence of his work. It is less surprising, however, when his writings are viewed in terms of their accessibility to scholars in various countries. None of the three works published in German-speaking countries (two of them in German and one in English) appeared in the most widely read of the central European geography serials. Furthermore, although his major work, the monograph in English on Alnwick,[3] appeared in one of the top half-dozen geographical serials in terms of international circulation, this was at a time when German geographers were apparently referring hardly at all to the English-language literature.[4] It would seem that the German–English language divide that obstructed the passage of urban morphological ideas out of central Europe in the inter-war period has in the post-war period acted as an effective barrier in the reverse direction for Conzen's ideas.

In considering the extension and development of Conzen's ideas four strands can be followed: first, work on town-plan analysis, a field in which Conzen established his pre-eminence in the early 1960s and that several scholars have entered since, but as yet without comparable success; secondly, the burgeoning literature on the fringe-belt concept, which if we are to judge by the verdict of other scholars must be deemed the most productive of the ideas that Conzen has developed; thirdly, the introduction to the study of those aspects of the urban landscape studied by Conzen of different approaches and techniques, including radically different approaches to both town-plan analysis and the fringe-belt concept; and finally, the largely unexplored potentialities of Conzen's approach to townscape management.

Extensions of town-plan analysis

During the last two decades there have been no published town-plan analyses of individual towns or cities comparable in conceptual richness and analytical depth to Conzen's studies of Alnwick and central Newcastle. The weight of scholarship that Conzen's studies demonstrated and their different intellectual perspective from work being undertaken in Britain or indeed other countries outside the German-speaking world may well have deterred potential emulators, and to this must be added the fact that in the 1960s geography in English-speaking countries was entering a phase of its development in which there was generally less interest in maps and landscapes. Furthermore, when there was a certain revival of interest in the landscape in the second half of the 1970s, the concern was more with the perception of the landscape than with its historical development. Although Straw attempted a thesis on the lines of the Alnwick study,[5] the study of the Scottish burgh of St Andrews by Brooks and Whittington is perhaps the nearest approach in the English-language literature of the last two decades to a major published analysis of the plan of an individual town.[6] The drawing of close parallels with the Alnwick study, however, would be misleading, since Brooks and Whittington tend to eschew the conceptualization of physical developments, deal only with the medieval period, and are concerned to a considerable extent with evaluating a "Bird's Eye View" of St Andrews. More generally conspicuous for its virtual absence in town-plan analyses since Conzen's study of central Newcastle has been the fringe-belt concept, despite its widespread examination in relation to land-use patterns. More representative of recent interest in the Conzenian tradition of town-plan analysis are two developments: first, attempts, almost for the first time in Britain, at comparative studies of towns over large areas, though generally below the national scale, and secondly analyses of burgages. To these may be added a weak but clearly detectable interest in Conzen's work among British historians and archaeologists.

Comparative studies

The studies of Alnwick and central Newcastle underlined the limitations of previous studies of town plans based on street systems. There was an evident need to employ Conzen's concepts and methods in comparative analyses. The problem has been that to study even a single town, unless it is very small, is a considerable undertaking in itself. The first attempt at a comparative study in Britain using Conzenian terminology was by Whitehand and Alauddin.[7] In attempting a preliminary survey of the whole of Scotland in respect of at least some aspects of all the major town-plan elements (street systems, plot patterns and building block-plans) this study served to emphasize the limited progress that was likely to be made without detailed analyses of individual plans:[8] even if town-plan classifications were infused with Conzenian concepts, without the combination in each town of ground survey, cartographic analysis and documentary evidence important matters were liable to be overlooked.

Slater has recently attempted a compromise by focussing on just two English counties, Warwickshire and Worcestershire, and restricting attention to two key elements in the town plan—market places and burgage series.[9] Limiting the field of investigation in this way still does not make it practicable to undertake a proper morphogenetic study of all towns in the study area, but his descriptive categorizations of market-place shapes are at least informed by selective information on origins and evolution and it is possible for him to put forward a tentative case for a relationship between the incidence of market colonization and the presence of ecclesiastical overlords. In the case of Slater's plot analyses, variations in Conzen's breadth to depth ratio for burgages would seem to be related to whether plots were laid out as part of a planned new town or developed from former village tofts and an association is noted between centrally-located narrower plots and greater subdivision.[10] Such investigations are at least beginning to rectify the striking gap in our knowledge of British town forms and their antecedence, but they are still largely descriptive studies informed by a detailed knowledge of Conzenian concepts. They are not a substitute for, and are not viable without, detailed morphogenetic analyses as demonstrated by Conzen.

Recognizing this Slater and Wilson have focused initial attempts at detailed comparative studies on the burgage,[11] recognized by Conzen as being of crucial importance as the basic "cell" of the medieval town plan. Such comparative work, added to a variety of detailed studies of burgages within individual towns, has justifiably brought the burgage to the forefront in the analysis of old established towns in Britain.

Burgage analysis

In recent years burgage analyses, especially attempts to reconstruct burgage patterns, have been undertaken in Britain using a variety of sources, including rentals,[12] court rolls,[13] and field and archaeological evidence.[14] Conzen's analyses of large-scale plans suggesting an original standard burgage width in Alnwick of 28–32 feet, revealed in survivals of this width and in such fractions and multiples of it as $0 \cdot 5$, $0 \cdot 75$, $1 \cdot 25$ and $1 \cdot 5$, have been followed up by Slater in the English midlands by analyses of modern plot frontages and an extension of this work to south-west England is now being undertaken.[15] The difficulty of obtaining plans for most towns that will permit measurements to a margin of error of one foot and the practical limitations on the large-scale reconstructions of burgage patterns based on archaeological evidence and documents is likely to make comparative work on medieval burgage patterns involving large numbers of towns at least partially dependent on this technique. Slater started by examining three street frontages in Stratford-upon-Avon, one of the few British towns in which an original standard burgage width (in this case 3·5 perches or 37·75 feet) is known to have existed. He found that the large majority of the plots had frontages that were 1·25, 0·75, 0·66, 0·5, 0·33 or 0·25 of the original frontage (using a margin of error of one foot each way) in those cases where they did not conform to that original frontage. Having established this relation between original medieval burgage widths and modern plots, two towns lacking documentation about their original plot dimensions were examined. In Shipston-on-Stour all but one-sixth of the plots in the medieval streets that were sampled had frontage widths with a clear relation to the 28–32 feet width discovered by Conzen in Alnwick[16] (and later by Brooks and Whittington in the western half of medieval St Andrews[17]) and interpreted by him as a possible reflection of the dimensions of a standard two-bay medieval eaves house. Furthermore, two such medieval houses could be erected on a burgage 3·5 perches wide, helping to explain both the initial choice of these dimensions and the subsequent mediation of burgages. In Pershore the frequency distribution of frontage widths, though showing little evidence of comparable regularities to those at Stratford and Shipston when the three measured plot series were taken together, was interpretable as two series representing major replanning (perhaps following a fire in 1233) and a third representing the vestiges of a different original standard width. Furthermore, the dimensions of the reconstituted burgage series, as at Stratford and Shipston, relate to the statute perch of 16·5 feet.

Although the three towns examined by Slater were all planned medieval towns and, being under monastic lordship, possibly subject to unusually close control, a convincing case is made for plot measurement and reconstruction as a method of establishing an outline pattern of development that could only be established otherwise from comprehensive documentation or by extensive archaeological excavation. In addition the method enables Conzen's hypothesis of a "standard" burgage width to be tested in towns whose archives lack the very large-scale early maps with which he worked. Differences between towns in the validity of this hypothesis can be established as well as regional or cultural variations in any "standard" that may exist.

Despite the growing interest in burgage patterns, the burgage cycle, which is undoubtedly one of Conzen's most important ideas, has received little more than passing reference in the literature. Carter in his study of Welsh towns refers to the link between the development from an "open" plan to one of solidly built-up central street blocks and the burgage cycle and notes that only the earliest stages of the cycle are apparent in the stunted and retarded towns.[18] Springett notes the applicability of the burgage cycle to the development of Huddersfield.[19] White-hand and Alauddin's estimates of building coverage for burgages in Scottish towns were undertaken with the burgage cycle in mind but they do not provide the quantitative data on how building coverages changed over time that are necessary for its proper consideration.[20] Straw is a rare exception in that he does examine central Nottingham in terms of the burgage cycle: his findings are broadly compatible with those of Conzen in central Newcastle but his study is a rather mechanical application of the framework provided by Conzen and conceptually adds nothing of significance.[21] The general absence of significant work on this topic would seem to be, at least in part, a reflection of the continuing lack of interest in concepts among urban historical geographers in English-speaking countries.

Related archaeological and historical studies

The long-term perpetuation of plot boundaries emphasized by Conzen has received support in archaeological excavations at Winchester and York,[22] and in the study of rentals at Canterbury.[23] In a more general way the international project for the publication of historical town plan atlases is to some extent rectifying the major deficiencies, especially in Britain, in knowledge of the topographical history of towns.[24] An important, if less conspicuous development is the gradual permeation of Conzen's ideas and methods into the local archaeological and historical literature. Notable examples are Bond's town-plan analysis of Pershore, which is particularly encouraging in its unusual sensitivity to the burgage pattern and its attempt to view specific detail in a comparative context,[25] and some aspects of the work of the Ludlow Historical Research Group.[26] The importance of the diffusion of Conzen's ideas to local groups, slow though it has been, is difficult to over-estimate. It is only as a result of detailed studies of individual towns and parts of towns by local scholars that it can possibly be practicable to build up a body of information that will form the basis for comparative studies and reduce the highly speculative element that necessarily characterizes present attempts to interpret town plans. The cost of such time-consuming local studies rules out the possibility of more than a modicum of funded research by universities or other bodies and the main role for professional geographers, historians and archaeologists in this field would seem to be the provision of integrative frameworks within which work in specific towns can be set.

It is not possible to refer here to all the recent work in urban history and archaeology that is relevant to Conzen's research. In a sense it would be misleading to do so, for, although Conzen's terminology and references to his work have in recent years appeared in the publications of historians and archaeologists,[27] when it comes to deeper consideration of concepts and methods the inter-disciplinary boundaries are almost as marked as they were in the 1960s. Yet there may have been sufficient recognition of some of the essentials of Conzen's work for future students of the town plan to view at least some of the findings of previous work with considerable caution. For example, the compositeness of even quite small plans, previously treated as entities, that Conzen has demonstrated has not gone unobserved by archaeologists.[28] It is to be hoped that this leads to a general wariness of the pitfalls of an earlier era of town-plan analysis in English-speaking countries in which so many of the lessons of research undertaken in central Europe were ignored.

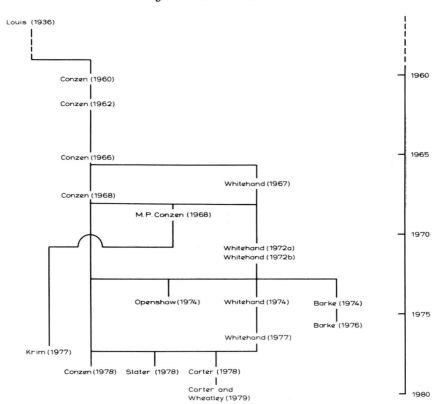

Figure 1. The development of fringe-belt research up to mid-1980. For works referred to see text.

Development of the fringe-belt concept

Conzen's development of the fringe-belt concept, arguably his most fundamental conceptual advance, has been largely ignored in recent contributions to town-plan analysis: this may be partly explained by the predominant concern in such contributions with medieval plans, for historical geographers concerned with the pre-industrial era have on the whole taken a particularly circumspect view of complex conceptualizations. Instead the fringe-belt concept has been developed mainly in research on land-use patterns—largely within the industrial era—the field in which it was originally formulated by Louis in 1936.[29] Studies concerned partially or wholly with the fringe-belt concept are shown by author and date in Fig. 1 in terms of the main lines of antecedence that may be discerned. Unpublished contributions are excluded, with the exception of one (a conference paper presented by M. P. Conzen in 1968[30]) that influenced a later contribution that did appear in print, as are non-original contributions such as recapitulations in text books. After Conzen's long-gestating studies that were eventually published in 1960[31] and 1962[32] it was not until the late 1960s that further studies appeared and ten of the eighteen studies ever published have appeared during the six-year period 1974 to 1979. During that time the number of authors has increased from four to ten, there being at least three others with research in progress at the end of that period.

In terms of the ideas developed and the approach adopted, fringe-belt studies may be grouped into three categories: first, traditional approaches that follow fairly closely the conceptions developed by Conzen in his studies of Alnwick and central Newcastle (in this category may be placed three of Conzen's own papers,[33] the paper already referred to by M. P. Conzen,[34] and the contributions by Whitehand (1967),[35] Krim (1977),[36] and Carter (1978)[37]); secondly, attempts to link this traditional conception with urban-rent theory (in this category may be placed the papers by Whitehand (1972a, b, 1974, 1977),[38] Openshaw (1974),[39] and Barke (1974, 1976)[40]); and thirdly, recent attempts to explore the connection between fringe belts and the family life cycle by Slater[41] and between fringe belts and the evolution of social areas by Carter and Wheatley.[42]

The traditional conception

In the English-speaking world of the early 1960s, when the models of Burgess and Hoyt were achieving widespread popularity among the growing community of urban geographers, the fringe-belt concept was a misfit. In its claims to recognition it had a number of impediments: first, its intellectual provenance was German at a time when in British geography links with America were increasingly replacing those with the continent of Europe;[43] secondly, it was primarily morphological at a time when the pendulum of fashion was swinging strongly towards a functional emphasis; thirdly, it was initially presented as an integral part of a specific town study and at first sight perhaps confusable with the studies of towns as unique entities that were falling out of favour; fourthly, at a time when there were increasing demands for theory its theoretical bases were by no means clear cut; fifthly, it was not readily amenable to quantification at a time when quantification was growing in popularity; sixthly, the distribution, mode of origin and heterogeneity of fringe belts made them much less amenable to rapid recognition either on the ground or on the map than the more homogeneous commercial, residential and industrial regions that characterized models current at the time; and finally, the information necessary for fringe-belt studies was by no means readily available, comparing most unfavourably in this respect with census data which were in addition much more amenable to the use of the computer.

It was not until 1967, five years after the publication of the study of central Newcastle, that a further publication appeared on the fringe-belt concept.[44] It is characteristic of the changes of fashion that had occurred by this time that, instead of treating fringe belts as an integral part of a wider town study, this paper by Whitehand examined them in their own right. The size of study area changed too, being the whole of a conurbation rather than an individual town, and the focus of interest was the land-use pattern rather than the town plan. The basic idea, the approach and the terminology, however, were similar to those employed in Conzen's studies of Alnwick and central Newcastle and the study served to confirm the utility of the fringe-belt concept as a means of putting order into the complex evolving form of urban areas. Its basic reliance on alternating phases of residential accretion and fringe-belt creation and the subsequent evolution of the zones thereby created was a fundamentally different conception from that of the models of Burgess and Hoyt and confusable with that of Burgess only in so far as the outcome on the ground tended to be roughly concentric in character. Nevertheless, even those researching in a field are sometimes guilty of recognizing superficial similarities, while ignoring fundamental differences, and with this in mind one of the points to which attention was drawn at the end of this study was the distinction between the CBD frame,[45] an American concept fashionable at the time and based essentially on the recognition of certain static land-use characteristics, and the inner fringe belt. This distinction illustrated the especial need for conceptual clarity where superficial visual similarity provides a false basis for synthesis. A problem that was not resolved, however, and one that greatly complicates the fringe-belt concept and has its parallels in other conceptions of the city based on a single centre, is that of the partial dependency of smaller centres on larger ones and hence the conceptual difficulty of dealing with the fringe belts of settlements that are in a sense themselves parts of the fringe belts of larger centres.

The next event in the development of the fringe-belt concept was a paper presented by M. P. Conzen, the son of M. R. G. Conzen, to the Annual Meeting of the Association of American Geographers West Lakes Division in 1968.[46] It was not a propitious time for the presentation of morphogenetic ideas to an American audience and this paper was to remain an isolated example of the application of the fringe-belt concept to America until Krim's much later work,[47] which was clearly influenced by it. Although M. P. Conzen's paper was never published, it contributed in a number of ways to the development of the fringe-belt concept. Not only did it illustrate for the first time its application to an American city (Madison, Wisconsin), but it was also the first attempt at a schematic representation of an urban area in terms of fringe-belt development. The application to Madison differed from previous studies in dealing with land uses that *theoretically* sought fringe sites, whether or not they actually located at the fringe.[48] It was especially important in providing empirical support for the hypothesis that fringe belts become consolidated over time by attracting compatible land uses. In terms of future research, it drew attention to the need to integrate the fringe-belt concept with general theories of urban and economic growth, a development that was still some years away.

A much wider dissemination of knowledge about the fringe-belt concept occurred in the 1970s, perhaps aided in 1972 by its appearance for the first time in a text book on urban geography,[49] and a much larger number of scholars became involved in its study. For the first time the study of a French town (Clermont-Ferrand) was undertaken,[50] and revealed the pronounced differences in pattern on the ground, though not in formative processes, that occurred where the onset of the industrial revolution was markedly retarded. In German-speaking Europe, however, there appeared no direct successors to Louis's original study of Berlin, despite the translation and development, albeit belatedly, of his idea in Britain, although there was no lack of appreciation of the significance of former fortifications in the present urban pattern,[51] the aspect of fringe belts with which Louis had been primarily concerned.

Within the traditional conception of the fringe belt, Carter, treating it as the critical concept in interpreting the outward extension of the built-up area,[52] became the second to use the fringe belt as a basis for schematizing urban internal structure diagrammatically, focussing on the industrial town in England and Wales between 1730 and 1900 and interweaving into his schema the development of the city centre and residential areas. But, as the concept has acquired wider currency, it is necessary to balance against such positive contributions as those of Carter misunderstandings not only of the fringe-belt concept as conceived by Conzen[53] but also of its subsequent usage[54] and of the type of investigation necessary to draw conclusions about its validity.[55] Nevertheless, in the main the 1970s were a period of constructive developments of the traditional conception, though some of these are inseparable from new conceptions, notably attempts to relate fringe belts first to building cycles and rent theory and secondly to social aspects.

Fringe belts, rent theory and building cycles

The roles of economic fluctuations and innovation and the relevance of the economics of location are implicit in Conzen's work of the 1960s rather than examined in themselves. One of the earliest clues to the interest that was to develop in the next decade in the role of economic fluctuations and innovation in fringe-belt development is in Conzen's own definition of a fringe belt in the glossary of technical terms added in 1969 to the reprinted version of the Alnwick study:

> "Significant changes in the whole civilizational context of a town's development such as fluctuations in population and economic development or repeated intensification in the introduction of all kinds of innovations causes intermittent deceleration or standstill in the outward growth of a town as well as marked changes in the admixture of new land-use types at the town fringe. In towns with a long history the geographical result emerging gradually from these dynamics is often a system of successive, broadly concentric fringe belts more or less separated by other, usually residential, integuments."[56]

What we do not get is any explicit mention of connections with rent theory, which in combination with economic (primarily building) fluctuations was soon to become a major line of investigation. This is not surprising since the Conzenian tradition is concerned with conceptualizing developments in the townscape in terms of an integrated historical context rather than with isolating and pursuing in detail a partial underlying mechanism. The deductive element that plays such an important part in the contructs of the urban-rent theorists is absent, at least in an explicit form, from the urban morphogenetic tradition, and its incorporation by Whitehand[57] represents the borrowing of ideas from the different intellectual environment of the American land economists.[58]

Whitehand's initial use of rent theory was only indirectly concerned with fringe belts.[59] Concerning himself with the spatial pattern of new land uses locating at the urban fringe, he focussed attention on the broad and heterogeneous category of institutional land uses that had been largely ignored by land economists. Noting their tendency to have linkages with the urban area that were weaker than those of housing areas and their comparatively large space requirements relative to their investments in building and other site improvements, he postulated that institutions would tend to have shallower bid-rent curves than residential developments and, *ceteris paribus*, less accessible locations. However, owing to the tendency for the creation of new institutional land uses to be less subject than housebuilding to large-scale long-term fluctuations, the bid-rent curve of institutions could be envisaged as sliding less far down the rent axis during housebuilding slumps, the creation of new institutional land uses thereby becoming more likely on sites that in times of a more buoyant land market and higher land values would have been utilized for housebuilding. The long-term outcome viewed in terms of a transect from city centre to rural fringe was for the admixture of new housing and new institutional developments to vary in much the same way as the alternating residential accretion and fringe-belt development envisaged by Conzen. The pattern of development in north-west Glasgow between 1840 and 1923 was found to be largely consistent with such a schema[60] and the idea of alternating periods of housebuilding boom and slump being associated more generally with variations in the intensity of new development was found to be consistent with the growth of a largely residential part of the fringe of west London between 1826 and 1869.[61] Parkes and Thrift subsequently presented in diagrammatic form a schematization of the relations between building cycles, land values, fringe-belt formation, and variations in the density of residential accretion.[62]

A natural extension of research on the urban fringe was the investigation of the changes that these fringe areas underwent when they became encompassed within the built-up area. Noting the similarity between fringe belts and zones with a high admixture of institutions, Whitehand focused attention on the fact that, although it had been well established that fringe belts not only tended to remain in existence for lengthy periods but, under certain circumstances, expanded into adjoining areas, the bid-rent mechanism as conceived up to that time implied that institutions would be displaced by housing in the next, or at least a subsequent, housebuilding boom.[63] He offered an explanation for this apparent anomaly in terms of the increases that tended to take place in the bid rents of institutions for their own and adjacent sites relative to those of housebuilders. These increases were related to the tendency for more capital to be invested over time in institutional sites than in housing sites and for the strength of the linkages between institutions and the urban area to increase as they became well established on their sites. At the same time, as institutions grew they tended to relocate those parts of their activities having weaker linkages to the urban area, for example sports fields, on cheaper land at the urban fringe. In this way locational decisions concerning different types of land use were effectively embodied within the decision-making of a single large organization, much as they were in the case of local government.[64]

The empirical basis for some of this reasoning about the evolution of fringe belts was scarcely more than impressionistic and the data required for a proper empirical examination are in most cases extremely time-consuming to acquire. However, certain aspects of the changes undergone by fringe belts after their initial establishment have been the subject of empirical studies. These have shown that it is not only institutions that are long-established on their sites that are able to compete successfully for internal sites. There may be a succession of similar uses on the same site, and, since there is a secular trend of rising land values, each tends to be more intensive than its predecessor.[65] Explanations that have been advanced for this include the fact that some of the assets accruing to a particular land use on a particular site, for example buildings and compatible environment, can be passed on to a related use.[66] This has been related to the displacement of some institutions to sites progressively farther from the city centre.[67] Barke made a special study of the sequence of land uses in fringe belts in the Scottish town of Falkirk and found considerable variations between both uses and locations relative to the town centre in their susceptibility to change.[68] He noted, for example, how certain sequences of change (for instance, the change from public open space to community buildings) were associated with continuity of ownership, especially where the owner was the local authority.

While these primarily empirical studies were going on, Openshaw was attempting to construct a theoretical framework on a more ambitious scale, in the belief that fringe-belt theory could provide "a unitary explanatory framework for the morphological and functional study of the townscape in a time extended framework".[69] He was concerned with both the formation phases of fringe-belt development and those of subsequent evolution as fringe belts became enveloped within a built-up area, but more notably he was interested in the functional linkages of fringe-belt land uses with other parts of the urban area. Broadening the scope from what he believed to have been an overconcern with the "medieval fringe-belt model",[70] in which developments are viewed in relation to a single-centre urban area with a long history, he felt the need to develop a more general model of the fringe-belt process that did not assume a specialized historical context and to show that the model was consistent with existing theories of urban economic structure.[71] In particular Openshaw drew attention to the significance of "fringe-belt cores", which might not only be central business cores, around which fringe belts develop.[72] He speculated on the process of morphological relocation associated with the decline in the functional significance of a fringe-belt core,[73] which could involve the "capture" of a fringe belt of a declining core by a growing one, the transfer of core and fringe-belt functions to a growing core and fringe belts, or the development of a declining inner fringe belt into an incipient middle fringe belt for a growing core.[74] Emphasis was placed on the various functional linkages that land uses within fringe belts might have—for example, distinguishing in the case of middle and outer fringe-belt uses between those linked to the urban area as a whole and those linked to local residential accretions.[75] The variety of functional links that a fringe belt might have in a large urban area was regarded as crucial, especially in a conurbation containing a number of centres, and Openshaw came to the conclusion that the location of fringe belts might not be related at all to the proximity of a town centre or to the economics of peripheral location. Inevitably his emphasis on changing functional linkages over lengthy periods of time makes his schema exceptionally demanding in the data requirements necessary for it to be tested, but the theoretical contribution that he has made is undoubtedly a major event in the history of fringe-belt research. The empirical challenge that it presents has yet to be taken up.

Openshaw's schema represented an attempt to construct a general theory of urban morphological development based on the fringe-belt concept after a period during which fringe belts had been abstracted from their place as an element in Conzen's view of morphological development and studied largely as separate entities from other morphological processes. This return to a more integrated view was re-emphasized in Whitehand's attempt to construct the basis for a historio-geographical theory of urban form which, although not couched explicitly in terms of fringe-belt development, bears a strong family resemblance in at least some of its facets to aspects of the fringe-belt concept.[76] The schema put forward integrates a variety of existing ideas relevant to the form of urban areas, but in particular connects, with varying degrees of directness, the processes of innovation and diffusion both with fluctuations in the amounts of urban development of different types and variations between land uses in their space and accessibility requirements. These relationships are extended to cover both intra- and inter-urban variations in form.

Other developments of the fringe-belt concept

With the recent proliferation of fringe-belt studies have come two noteworthy departures from the traditional and rent-theory approaches. The first was introduced by Slater in 1978[77] and the second by Carter and Wheatley in 1979.[78]

Slater augmented the fringe-belt concept as it had become widely accepted by 1978, especially its conception in primarily economic terms, by examining the relationship between the timing of the creation, modification and redevelopment of a single category of fringe-belt land use—the nineteenth-century ornamental villa—and significant stages in the life cycle of the occupants. The stage reached in the family life cycle was a significant factor in determining the timing of the adjustment of the landscape to changing intra-urban location and more general economic climate. Marriage was in this respect the most significant event and in large towns generations of villas occupying fringe belts successively farther from the town centre could be envisaged as resulting from the consequent new household formation,[79] though in a small country town a sequence of additions to a single nineteenth-century fringe belt was more likely. The other significant event to "trigger" change was the death of a villa owner, which in particular provided opportunity for changes to an existing villa—notably, change of tenure, renovation of the buildings, extension of the grounds, change of use and, the greatest change of all, redevelopment. The townscape is thus viewed primarily as the outcome of an interaction of land economics and family life cycles, and some of the unexplained residuals in a purely economic conception of fringe-belt development are thereby explained.

Carter and Wheatley's contribution is like Slater's in its exploration of the relationship between fringe-belt development and social considerations, but differs from it in being concerned with social areas rather than individual families. Particular attention is given to fixation lines, to which Conzen had attached so much importance in his studies of Alnwick and central Newcastle. Fringe belts provide the basis for the evolution of the physical structure of the urban area, which is then related to the evolution of the distribution pattern of social classes. The accent is on the integration of fringe-belt development with other aspects of urban change. It is the first major attempt to introduce the development of social areas into fringe-belt studies but it is characteristic of the recent tendency to treat fringe belts in a less technical manner and to establish a cross-fertilization with other aspects of urban geographical research.

Changes of approach and technique

The way in which the fringe-belt concept has been developed over the last 20 years has reflected a rapidly changing intellectual environment. Out of this changing environment have come more general changes of approach and technique within urban morphology. Conzen's major works on Alnwick and central Newcastle were contemporary with the early stages of the quantitative and theoretical revolution in geography. Indeed, at the International Geographical Union symposium in urban geography held at Lund in 1960, when the central Newcastle paper was first presented, criticism of urban morphology for its lack of theory was voiced, although unfortunately much of the discussion was neither as discriminating nor as informed as the complexity of the issues warranted.[80] Especially apparent at this symposium was the strong tide that was running in America towards the widespread application of quantitative methods. In the light of the interests of American urban geographers it is not surprising that these applications were to the functional aspects of the subject. But it was natural enough that as such methods were more widely adopted elsewhere attempts were made to subject to quantitative analysis all the major townscape elements distinguished by Conzen and to make more explicit the role of deductive constructs in urban morphology. This occurred mainly, but by no means exclusively, in Britain, where a largely descriptive urban morphology had continued to attract adherents during the 1950s.[81]

In the study of building types, early attempts at statistical analysis were those of Corey,[82] Davies,[83] and Johnston,[84] followed later by Openshaw.[85] Conzen had, of course, brought measurement to the fore in urban morphology, especially in his work on plot dimensions and building coverage, but it was not until 1968 that the first example of the use of statistical analytical procedures in the geographical study of the building fabric appeared in a major journal, in Davies's calculation of the correlation between indices of the form and function of commercial centres in the Rhondda–Pontypridd area of South Wales.[86] This was quickly followed by Johnston's use of non-parametric analyses of variance to test diffusion models of the intra-urban development of house types.[87] Such simple statistical tests are now widely acknowledged to be useful in the analysis of the building fabric,[88] but it is doubtful whether this is true of some of the applications of multivariate statistics.

The most ambitious use of multivariate analysis to date is Openshaw's factor analytical study of field observations of 169 attributes of buildings for the whole of the Tyneside town of South Shields.[89] As a result of this study Openshaw expresses doubts, on the basis of the descriptive characteristics of buildings that he employs, about the emphasis placed on morphological periods in previous studies—notably in Conzen's research, which in other respects has been a major influence on his work. Indeed, he goes so far as to suggest that continued use of "period models" may be an obstacle to the further advancement of research in urban morphology,[90] but it should be emphasized that, for the moment at least, this remains an isolated view, the justification for which is open to serious question. He also believes that the morphological regions objectively recognized as a result of his study could not have been closely approximated by traditional map analysis, which would in any case not have been practicable with so many morphological characteristics being considered.

Carter has expressed reservations about the justification for such complex statistical procedures, and is of the opinion that regionalizations arrived at in this way will accord fairly closely with those based on much simpler methods.[91] Corey had in fact earlier employed principal components analysis to identify the major dimensions of variability among house types and used the resultant dimensions as a basis for deriving regionalizations. Using information from the real property records of the Auditor of Hamilton County, Ohio, component scores based on 40 variables recorded for 250 individual houses in a neighbourhood of Cincinnati were grouped using a stepwise aggregation program and the resultant groupings were mapped and house-type regions identified.[92] The labour of collecting the data necessary for such studies is considerable, especially in Britain where an element of field work is indispensable. But useful results can emerge, as Forster demonstrated in his study of the physical characteristics of bye-law housing in Hull using association analysis to tackle the problem of grouping.[93] In this case an equally important contribution, and one that is relevant to Whitehand's attempt to formulate a theory of urban form founded in part on the interrelationship of building cycles and innovation,[94] is the examination of the relationship between building cycles and bye-law cycles, suggesting that although the two cycles might be independent of one another, their periodical interaction produced the most spectacular periods of change in the development of the form of court housing in Hull.[95]

In studies of the town plan, an early attempt at quantification using analysis of variance was that of Johnston in his investigation of the development of Melbourne's street pattern.[96] This was followed in the 1970s by attempts by Openshaw and Millward to use statistical measures to describe actual plan elements. Openshaw employs ten different measures of shape in his examination of building block-plans and plot characteristics in South Shields, the problem of obtaining numerical descriptions being solved by digitizing the outlines of the plots and block-plans.[97] As in his analysis of building types, he draws attention to the lack of homogeneity within morphological periods and the presence of similar forms in different morphological periods. Millward, in a comparative study of Canadian and English cities, also uses quantitative measures of plan elements. For example, he analyses the street system in terms of road density, road junction frequency, road connectivity, angular deviation at junctions and road curvature.[98] He claims that his work "builds on the notion of plan-generality put forward by Conzen",[99] but his approach is quite different. His use of distance from the city centre as a surrogate for time of development, the employing of map scales as small as 1/63 360 for analysis, and the importance attached to the sampling of small areas of street layout, are far removed from the genetic subtleties of town-plan analysis in the Conzenian tradition.

The problem with the measures employed by Millward, as with the application of measures of shape employed in other fields to plan analysis to which Carter has drawn attention,[100] and most of which Openshaw has employed,[101] is harnessing them to actual morphological problems, which tend to be intractable to such mechanistic treatment. Carter's paper at the conference organized by the Council for British Archaeology in 1974 on medieval plans and topography prompted critical comments from Conzen on the appropriateness of the suggested applications of such techniques and few of the historians and archaeologists present were convinced that quantitative methods in general had much to offer them, at least for the study of medieval town plans.[102] The reaction to statistical techniques at that conference exemplifies the developing tension in the 1970s between social scientists, such as Openshaw and Millward, who see the future of urban morphology as involving the storage and manipulation of large data sets and related to advances in statistical techniques, information systems and computer hardware,[103] and scholars with strong leanings towards history, such as Slater and Bond for whom the very nature of urban morphology, with its concern for regional and historical variety and its considerable dependence on unique documentary sources, renders it a task for individual scholarship rather than the large-scale application of technology. Clearly the two camps tend to have rather different aims and arguments over method and technique are liable to prove fruitless unless this is understood.

A related controversy surrounds attempts that have been made to introduce deductive strategies into urban morphology in an explicit way, the use of a bid-rent construct to investigate urban fringe development being an example that has already been discussed. These involve the introduction of major simplifying assumptions and the disaggregation of processes in terms of individual economic or social variables with a specified relationship to each other. The explicit use of these procedures is foreign to the morphogenetic tradition and attempts to recast Conzen's work in these terms are thwart with difficulties. More feasible, though not without danger of misrepresentation, is the re-phrasing of some of Conzen's statements for the purposes of empirical testing, and Barke's use of a transition matrix to examine land-use succession in fringe belts is an example of the type of quantitative analysis that can be accomplished by working directly from a Conzenian idea.[104] But any attempt to relate Conzen's ideas to constructs developed in an explicitly deductive manner requires, it would seem, a different approach. In the only attempt to date, theory construction proceeded by deduction from essentially economic or economico-geographical relationships and then after the resultant theory had been examined in a test area, the results were considered in relation to Conzen's ideas.[105] This procedure, discussed briefly in the previous section of this chapter, has cast new light on processes identified by Conzen.

Attempts to look at Conzenian concepts in this way do not, of course, provide an answer to those who have criticized Conzen's work for its lack of direct consideration of the decision-making that underlies developments in the urban landscape.[106] Carter, in his concern for a decision-making approach has suggested that the development of town plans might be presented in terms of the degree of concentration of decision-making rather than in terms of historical periods.[107] He illustrates this by showing the basic similarities in form between Caernarvon, a medieval bastide, and Merthyr Tydfil, a creation of the industrial period. Such an approach departs fundamentally from the morphogenetic tradition. There is no reason, however, why attention to decision-making should not play a role within an approach to the townscape that retains a historical framework. Indeed, studies of the building fabric of selected British town centres are now in progress that examine the roles of architects, builders, developers, building owners, and building users in the historical development of the townscape.[108]

Urban landscape management

Whereas it is justifiable to speak of a Conzenian school in discussing research on the development of the urban landscape, and within fringe-belt research alone it is possible to construct a sizable family tree of the developments that have taken place, the same certainly cannot be said about Conzen's ideas on townscape conservation. Even the idea of townscape "management" as distinct from "preservation" is still rarely encountered in Britain. Indicative of the comparative neglect of this aspect of Conzen's work is the fact that the *Social Science Citation Index*, from 1966 to 1979 inclusive, lists only two references to "Historical townscapes in Britain" (Chapter 3), compared with 26 to *Alnwick*, and only one to "Geography and townscape conservation" (Chapter 4), although it should be remembered that the latter was only published in 1975.[109] This was in spite of a major growth of interest in the preservation of the built environment during this period.[110]

It is interesting to note the quite different impact of a parallel contribution in timing and in some respects derivation: that of Linton on landscape evaluation. Linton, an exact contemporary of Conzen, also late in his career brought together life-long morphological and aesthetic interests, devising a basis for producing Scenic Resources Maps in a paper which quickly became a significant landmark in the development of the field of landscape evaluation.[111] Again taking the *Social Science Citation Index* as a crude measure of a paper's impact, sixteen references to this paper were recorded during the years 1969 to 1979 inclusive.

The comparative lack of impact of Conzen's ideas on townscape conservation becomes more understandable if the nature, derivation and circumstances of publication are considered. The ideas themselves derive from his own ideas on the nature of the townscape, particularly as expounded in the late 1950s and early 1960s. They represent the integration of Conzen's artistic and historical interests and are only completely meaningful if viewed in the context of his earlier morphogenetic concepts. This complex derivation combined with the fact that the ideas initially appeared in publications that were not widely available has undoubtedly contributed to the comparatively little attention they have hitherto received from other scholars. Furthermore, whereas Linton's ideas on landscape evaluation were confined to the aesthetic dimension, Conzen's on townscape management involved the additional dimensions of practical utility and, more importantly, appeal to the intellect. He was thus placing the evaluation of the urban landscape on a much more complex plane and, whereas Linton offers a finished and quantitative basis for assessing landscapes, Conzen provides no such neat package. He leaves us in no doubt that much of the underlying theoretical work remains to be done and provides only guide lines by which conservation strategies may be derived, emphasizing the need for a comprehensive morphogenetic theory of towns that can form the basis for a theory of townscape management and expressing doubts as to whether a quantitative approach to conservation will be possible.

Yet there are some clear indications as to priorities and procedures for the geographer, or indeed town planner, concerned with conservation of the urban landscape. Most importantly, the key to informed townscape management is understanding of how the townscape has evolved. The Conzenian townscape is a stage on which successive societies work out their lives, each society learning from, and working to some extent within the framework provided by, the experiments of its predecessors. Viewed in this way townscapes represent accumulated experience, old-established townscapes especially so, and are thus a precious asset. This asset is threefold. First, it has practical utility at the most basic level in providing orientation: our mental map and therefore the efficiency with which we function spatially is dependent on our recognition of the identity of localities. Secondly, it has intellectual value by helping both individual and society to orientate in time: through its high density of forms a well-established townscape provides a particularly strong visual experience of the history of an area, helping the individual to place himself within a wider evolving society, stimulating historical comparison and thus providing a more informed basis for reasoning. Thirdly, and more contentiously, the combination of forms created by the piecemeal adaptation, modification and replacement of elements in old-established townscapes has aesthetic value: for example, in the maintenance of human scale, in the visual impact of and orientation provided by dominant features in the townscape, such as churches and castles, and in the stimulus to the imagination and the visual surprises provided by variations in street width and orientation. Clearly all three assets are interrelated and emotional and aesthetic experiences are particularly tightly intertwined with, though not necessarily dependent on, appreciation of historical and geographical significance.

If a key concept for future research is to be singled out from Conzen's papers on townscape management, then prime consideration must be given to the townscape as the objectivation of the spirit of a society, viewed not at a moment in time but as a historical phenomenon. As change after change takes place on the ground, consisting of additions, modifications and subtractions, but invariably related in some degree to what was there before, the townscape encapsulates the history of a society in a particular locale.[112] The variation between townscapes in their historical expressiveness, provides a basis for determining conservation priorities. An important aspect of this, and the most important contribution of geographical townscape analysis, is the identification of townscape units as a framework for establishing the nature and intensity of the historical expressiveness of various parts of a town.

Although the recommended procedures remain to be taken up directly, the underlying sensitivity to the urban landscape and concern for its sympathetic management revealed in this aspect of Conzen's work fortunately has its echo well beyond the geographical profession. In a criticism of the lack of attention to detail of which the planning and architectural professions have been guilty too frequently, Allsop writes:

"We have lost the technique of adding and adapting. We are obsessed by the bulldozer and thinking big. We have lost the art of fitting the new into the old, of maintaining the sense of place and continuity which is so important for people. We need to learn the art of graceful transition."[113]

And on the wider significance of the urban landscape Banz writes: "Urban form can give man a sense of involvement in time beyond his own life-span and in space beyond his immediate grasp."[114] But these are perceptive scholars able to stand back from the problem; the task of educating a wider population has scarcely begun.

Conclusion and prospect

Though many of Conzen's ideas remain to be taken up, especially in the field of townscape management, the last 20 years have witnessed, rather belatedly, the development of a Conzenian school within urban morphology. This has taken place to a large extent within a rather unpropitious British environment and at some distance both physically and intellectually from the main action in contemporary geography. But it has not been uninfluenced by the major developments in English-language geography that have emanated from America, some of which have stimulated attempts to view Conzenian concepts in a different light. The roots of the Conzenian tradition, however, are firmly in central Europe in the inter-war period and earlier. The contrasts with the artistic approach to the British townscape of Johns,[115] or the much more eclectic morphogenetic approach of Vance are considerable.[116] The contrasts with the work of rare landscape historians like Hoskins[117] and Beresford,[118] who largely eschew analytical concepts, are even more pronounced and to some extent reflect the isolation of historians from geographical research. Indeed only a single reference by a historian or economic historian to any of Conzen's work appears in the *Social Science Citation Index* 1966–79; a remarkable fact, even allowing for the limited range of source works upon which that publication is based.

The fact that we can without great difficulty trace back the origins of the Conzenian tradition to the end of the nineteenth century and that the antecedence is in major respects, though by no means entirely, indigenous to geography, makes it atypical of present-day urban geography in English-speaking countries, which is undergoing a period of direct borrowing from the social sciences on an unprecedented scale. This borrowing may well partly reflect the weak conceptual base that urban geography in the English-speaking world inherited from earlier decades when it was poorly connected both to other disciplines and to indigenous developments on the continent of Europe. The Conzenian tradition, in contrast, has drawn heavily on a conceptually more developed and secure foundation that was created within geography in the German-speaking countries in the inter-war period and earlier. Thus, despite attempts at integration, it is not surprising that its concepts appear distinctive in an environment dominated by recent borrowings from the social sciences, in particular as they have developed in America.

The distinction between indigenous concepts and imported methods is useful in reviewing recent developments in the Conzenian tradition. Whereas with direct attempts to follow Conzen's work on town-plan analysis and fringe belts a strong element of continuity between studies can be observed, attempts to apply statistics in urban morphology have on the whole been characterized by individual forays into the field, perhaps incidental to some other purpose. The element of continuity in town-plan analysis and fringe-belt studies reflects both the long-term interest that a few scholars have maintained in urban morphology and the direct attempts by a small number of new entrants to the field to build on existing work. In contrast those who adopted a statistical approach to urban morphology in their initial research tended to move quickly into new, often functional, fields, better endowed with quantifiable data. This is certainly true of Johnston and Davies at the end of the 1960s and Forster and Openshaw in the early 1970s. While threads can be detected linking certain conceptual developments within British urban morphology in the 1960s and 1970s, with Conzen's role being central, technical and methodological developments in the field largely reflect an intermittent backwash from the major waves of influence from other disciplines, especially economics and statistics, that were impinging on other aspects of geography.

The prospects for building further on the Conzenian tradition seem to be brighter now than for some time. A major attempt is being made by a group of British researchers at the University of Birmingham to integrate the analysis of changes to the building fabric with the study of the individuals and organizations involved in the various aspects of property development, notably building users, developers and architects. This research, and allied work in the field of town-plan analysis, is basically in sympathy with the main tenets of the Conzenian approach as it has developed over the post-war decades. It adopts the individual plot as the unit of analysis and exploits the potentialities of local authority building plans and registers, which were used earlier by Conzen himself in his study of Alnwick and subsequently by among others Dyos,[119] Openshaw [120] and Aspinall.[121] The building plans and registers, though by no means a problem-free source for the researcher, provide the basis for the period since the middle of the nineteenth century for an approach in which the townscape is examined in conjunction with a study of those making the decisions that affect it.[122] Furthermore, although they vary from one authority to another in detail and in the periods for which they are extant, they make more feasible the larger-scale data collecting and processing desired by Openshaw.[123]

In this same line of research there is also considerable scope for developing further and testing Conzen's ideas on townscape management. Here the practical aspects of implementing Conzen's approach are as yet poorly worked out. An integrated study of the town plan, building fabric and land and building utilization is a prerequisite, but in practice these three elements have tended to be the subject of separate investigations. Published examples of their integration are confined to the Whitby study[124] and the abbreviated studies reprinted in this volume (Chapters 3 and 4). A major practical step would be to investigate the theoretical and practical problems of effecting for a sample of historic towns a comparison of theoretical developments based on Conzenian principles with actual developments; for instance, for the post-war period. Since local authority building plans would be as important as a source for this work as they are in the attempts to develop morphological theory through the integrated study of the building fabric and agencies involved in property development, there are practical as well as theoretical advantages in combining fundamental and applied research.

An optimistic view of this most recent extension of urban morphological research is encouraged by revivals of interest in the urban landscape reported elsewhere,[125] notably in America where recent approaches to preservation reveal a sympathy with the urban landscape[126] that would have been rare only a decade ago. In the light of this increasing awareness there is a good prospect that attempts to co-ordinate research efforts will succeed in putting on a more secure logistic footing a line of research that, but for a small number of strategic publications by Conzen during the 1950s and 1960s, would have been almost snuffed out.

Notes

1. Conzen, M. R. G. (1970) "The purpose and contents of geography", *Univ. of Newcastle upon Tyne Dep. Geogr. Semin. Pap.* 14.

2. In addition to the research works discussed in this chapter there are a variety of books, most of them intended for a less specialized readership, that contain sections on Conzen's work: for example, Johns, E. (1965) *British townscapes* (London) pp. 45–7; Schwarz, G. (1966) *Allgemeine Siedlungsgeographie* 3rd edn (Berlin) pp. 13, 537; Carter, H. (1972) *The study of urban geography* (London) pp. 138, 140–1, 157; Aston, M. and Bond, J. (1976) *The landscape of towns* (London) pp. 18, 98–9; Burke, G. (1976) *Townscapes* (Harmondsworth) pp. 120–1; Vance, J. E. (1977) *This scene of man: the role and structure of the city in the geography of western civilization* (New York) pp. 121, 125–6.

3. Conzen, M. R. G. (1960) *Alnwick, Northumberland: a study in town-plan analysis* Inst. Br. Geogr. Publ. No. 27.

4. Whitehand, J. W. R. and Edmondson, P. M. (1977) "Europe and America: the reorientation in geographical communication in the post-war period", *Prof. Geogr.* **29**, 278–82.

5. Straw, F. I. (1967) "An analysis of the town plan of Nottingham: a study in historical geography", unpubl. M.A. thesis, Univ. of Nottingham.

6. Brooks, N. P. and Whittington, G. (1977) "Planning and growth in the medieval Scottish burgh: the example of St Andrews", *Trans. Inst. Br. Geogr.* **2**, 278–95. For another recent attempt at the analysis of the plan of an individual city see Simms, A. (1979) "Medieval Dublin: a topographical analysis", *Irish Geogr.* **12**, 25–41.

7. Whitehand, J. W. R. and Alauddin, K. (1969) "The town plans of Scotland: some preliminary considerations", *Scott. geogr. Mag.* **85**, 109–21.

8. Ibid. p. 21.

9. Slater, T. R. (1981) "Urban genesis and medieval town plans in Warwickshire and Worcestershire", in Slater, T. R. and Jarvis, P. J. (eds) *Field and forest: an historical geography of Warwickshire and Worcestershire* (Norwich).

10. See also Meeson, R. A. (1979) "The formation of Tamworth", unpubl. M.A. thesis, Univ. of Birmingham, pp. 66–72, 124–7.

11. See, for example, Slater, T. R. and Wilson, C. (1977) *Archaeology and development in Stratford-upon-Avon* (Birmingham) pp. 9–10, and especially Slater, T. R. (1980) "The analysis of burgages in medieval towns", *Dep. Geogr. Univ. of Birmingham Wking. Pap.* 4.

12. Urry, W. (1967) *Canterbury under the Angevin kings* (London).

13. Meeson, op. cit. (note 10).

14. Brooks and Whittington, op. cit. (note 6). Keene, D. J. (1974) "Some aspects of the history, topography and archaeology of the north-eastern part of the medieval city of Winchester with special reference to the Brooks area", unpubl. D.Phil. thesis, Univ. of Oxford, uses a variety of sources (notably deeds, account rolls, court rolls, maps and

archaeological evidence) to reconstruct part of the medieval city of Winchester but is only incidentally concerned with plots.

15. Slater (1980) op. cit. (note 11).

16. Conzen (1960) op. cit. pp. 32–4 (note 3).

17. Brooks and Whittington, op. cit. p. 288 (note 6).

18. Carter, H. (1965) *The towns of Wales: a study in urban geography* (Cardiff) p. 205.

19. Springett, R. J. (1979) "The mechanics of urban land development in Huddersfield 1770–1911", unpubl. Ph.D. thesis, Univ. of Leeds, p. 83.

20. Whitehand and Alauddin, op. cit. pp. 114–15 (note 7).

21. Straw, op. cit. (note 5).

22. Webster, L. E. and Cherry, J. (eds) (1977) "Medieval Britain in 1976", *Medieval Archaeol.* **21**, 248.

23. Urry, op. cit. pp. 191–2 (note 12).

24. Lobel, M. D. (ed.) (1969 and 1975) *Historic towns: maps and plans of towns and cities in the British Isles, with historical commentaries, from earliest times to about 1800* (London) Vols I and II. For a review of this and of the corresponding publications in Germany and Scandinavia see Hall, T. and Borgwik, L. (1978) "Urban-history atlases: a survey of recent publications", *Särtr. hist. Tidskr.* Conzen is a member of the committee, mainly comprised of historians, set up to supervise the preparation of the British volumes. The project was initiated by a sub-committee set up by the International Congress of Historians in 1955 to promote the study of medieval towns—see Conzen, M. R. G. (1968) "The use of town plans in the study of urban history", in Dyos, H. J. (ed.) *The study of urban history* (London) esp. pp. 113–14.

25. Bond, C. J. (1977) "The topography of Pershore", in Bond, C. J. and Hunt, A. M. (eds) "Recent archaeological work in Pershore", *Vale of Evesham hist. Soc. Res. Pap.* **6**, 18–26.

26. See, for example, Speight, M. E. and Lloyd, D. J. (1978) *Ludlow houses and their residents* Ludlow Res. Pap. 1 (Birmingham) p. 2, footnote 2, and Lloyd, D. and Moran, M. (n.d.) *The corner shop* Ludlow Res. Pap. 2 (Birmingham).

27. See, for example, Addyman, P. V. (1977) "York and Canterbury as ecclesiastical centres", in Barley, M. W. (ed.) *European towns: their archaeology and early history* (London) p. 503; Platt, C. (1976) "The evolution of towns: natural growth", in Barley, M. W. (ed.) *The plans and topography of medieval towns in England and Wales* Counc. Br. Archaeol. 14, p. 53; Palliser, D. M. (1976) "Sources for urban topography: documents, buildings, and archaeology", in Barley (1976) op. cit. p. 3; Biddle, M. (1976) "The evolution of towns: planned towns before 1066", in Barley (1976) op. cit. p. 20.

28. See, for example, Butler, L. (1976) "The evolution of towns: planted towns after 1066", in Barley (1976), op. cit. p. 32 (note 27).

29. Louis, H. (1936) "Die geographische Gliederung von Gross-Berlin", *Länderkundliche Forschung* Krebs-Festschrift, 146–71.

30. Conzen, M. P. (1968) "Fringe location land uses: relict patterns in Madison, Wisconsin", unpubl. paper presented to the 19th Annual Meeting of the Association of American Geographers West Lakes Division, Madison, Wisconsin.

31. Conzen (1960) op. cit. (note 3).

32. See Chapter 2.

33. See Chapters 3 and 5 and Conzen (1968) op. cit. p. 122 (note 24).

34. Conzen, M. P. op. cit. (note 30).

35. Whitehand, J. W. R. (1967) "Fringe belts: a neglected aspect of urban geography", *Trans. Inst. Br. Geogr.* **41**, 223–33.

36. Krim, A. J. (1977) *Survey of architectural history in Cambridge. Report five: northwest Cambridge* (Cambridge, Mass.) esp. pp. 18–25.

37. Carter, H. (1978) "Towns and urban systems 1730–1900", in Dodgshon, R. A. and Butlin, R. A. (eds) *An historical geography of England and Wales* (London) pp. 367–400.

38. Whitehand, J. W. R. (1972a) "Building cycles and the spatial pattern of urban growth", *Trans. Inst. Br. Geogr.* **56**, 39–55; Whitehand, J. W. R. (1972b) "Urban-rent theory, time series and morphogenesis: an example of eclecticism in geographical research", *Area* **4**, 215–22; Whitehand, J. W. R. (1974) "The changing nature of the urban fringe: a time perspective", in Johnson, J. H. (ed.) *Suburban growth: geographical processes at the edge of the western city* (London) pp. 31–52; Whitehand, J. W. R. (1977) "The basis for an historico-geographical theory of urban form", *Trans. Inst. Br. Geogr.* N.S. **2**, 400–16.

39. Openshaw, S. (1974a) "A theory of the morphological and functional development of the townscape in a historical context", *Univ. of Newcastle upon Tyne Dep. Geogr. Semin. Pap.* **24**.

40. Barke, M. (1974) "The changing urban fringe of Falkirk: some morphological implications of urban growth", *Scott. geogr. Mag.* **90**, 85–97; Barke, M. (1976) "Land use succession: a factor in fringe-belt modification", *Area* **8**, 303–6.

41. Slater, T. R. (1978) "Family, society and the ornamental villa on the fringes of English country towns", *J. hist. Geogr.* **4**, 129–44.

42. Carter, H. and Wheatley, S. (1979) "Fixation lines and fringe belts, land uses and social areas: nineteenth-century change in the small town", *Trans. Inst. Br. Geogr.* N.S. **4**, 214–38.

43. Whitehand and Edmondson, op. cit. (note 4).

44. Whitehand (1967) op. cit. (note 35).

45. Horwood, E. M. and Boyce, R. R. (1959) *Studies of the central business district and urban freeway development* (Seattle) pp. 15–22.

46. Conzen, M. P. op. cit. (note 30).

47. Krim, op. cit. (note 36).

48. Part of the antecedence of this approach is to be found in Colby, C. C. (1933) "Centrifugal and centripetal forces in urban geography", *Ann. Ass. Am. Geogr.* **23**, 1–20.

49. Carter (1972) op. cit. pp. 140–1, 289 (note 2).

50. Whitehand (1974) op. cit. pp. 44–5 (note 38).

51. Lichtenberger, E. (1970) "The nature of European urbanism", *Geoforum* **4**, 52–3.

52. Carter (1978) op. cit. p. 389 (note 37).

53. Jackson, J. T. (1977) "Housing and social structure in mid-Victorian Wigan and St Helens", unpubl. Ph.D. thesis, Univ. of Liverpool, p. 6.

54. Lea, K. J. (1980) "Greater Glasgow", *Scott. geogr. Mag.* **96**, 14–15.

55. Homan, R. and Rowley, G. (1980) "The location of institutions during the process of urban growth: a case study of churches and chapels in nineteenth-century Sheffield", *E. Midld Geogr.* **7**, 150.

56. Conzen, M. R. G. (1969) *Alnwick, Northumberland: a study in town-plan analysis* Inst. Br. Geogr. Publ. No. 27, reprint, p. 125. This reprinted version is virtually identical to the original edition (note 3), published in 1960, except for the addition of a glossary of technical terms.

57. Whitehand (1972a) op. cit. (note 38).

58. For example, Alonso, W. (1960) "A theory of the urban land market", *Pap. reg. Sci. Ass.* **6**, 156.

59. Whitehand (1972a) op. cit. (note 38).

60. Ibid.

61. Whitehand, J. W. R. (1975) "Building activity and intensity of development at the urban fringe: the case of a London suburb in the nineteenth century", *J. hist. Geogr.* **1**, 211–24. For a much broader compilation of data on this and related subjects see Whitehand, J. W. R. (1981) "Fluctuations in the land-use composition of urban development during the industrial era", *Erdkunde* **35**, 129–40.

62. Parkes, D. N. and Thrift, N. J. (1980) *Times, spaces and places: a chronogeographic perspective* (Chichester) p. 427.

63. Whitehand (1972b) op. cit. (note 38).

64. Ibid.

65. Whitehand (1974) op. cit. pp. 48–9 (note 38); Barke (1976) op. cit. (note 40).

66. Whitehand (1974) op. cit. p. 48 (note 38).

67. Ibid. p. 49.

68. Barke (1976) op. cit. (note 40).

69. Openshaw (1974a) op. cit. p. 20 (note 39).

70. Ibid. p. 6.

71. Ibid. p. 7.

72. Ibid. pp. 8–9.

73. Ibid. p. 14.

74. Ibid. p. 13.

75. Ibid. p. 16.

76. Whitehand (1977) op. cit. (note 38).

77. Slater (1978) op. cit. (note 41).

78. Carter and Wheatley op. cit. (note 42).

79. Slater (1978) op. cit. p. 139 (note 41).

80. Norborg, K. (ed.) (1962) *Proceedings of the IGU symposium in urban geography Lund 1960* (Lund) pp. 462–9.

81. For example, Thurston, H. S. (1953) "The urban regions of St Albans", *Trans. Inst. Br. Geogr.* **19**, 107–21; Smailes, A. E. (1955) "Some reflections on the geographical description and analysis of townscapes", *Trans. Inst. Br. Geogr.* **21**, 99–115; Stedman, M. B. (1958) "The townscape of Birmingham in 1956", *Trans. Inst. Br. Geogr.* **25**, 225–38; Jones, E. (1958) "The delimitation of some urban landscape features in Belfast", *Scott. geogr. Mag.* **74**, 150–62; Carter, H. (1958) "Aberystwyth: the modern development of a medieval castle town in Wales", *Trans. Inst. Br. Geogr.* **25**, 239–53.

82. Corey, K. E. (1969) "A spatial analysis of urban houses", unpubl. Ph.D. diss., Univ. of Cincinnati.

83. Davies, W. K. D. (1968) "The morphology of central places: a case study", *Ann. Ass. Am. Geogr.* **58**, 91–110.

84. Johnston, R. J. (1969) "Towards an analytical study of the townscape: the residential building fabric", *Geogr. Annlr.* Ser. B, **51**, 20–32.

85. Openshaw, S. (1974b) "Processes in urban morphology with special reference to South Shields", unpubl. Ph.D. thesis, Univ. of Newcastle upon Tyne.

86. Davies, op. cit. p. 101 (note 83).

87. Johnston, op. cit. p. 26 (note 84).

88. See Fennell, R. I. and Openshaw, S. (1971) "Fieldwork perception in the period

dating of urban buildings", *J. geogr. Soc. Univ. of Newcastle upon Tyne* **19**, 19–23; Whitehand, J. W. R. (1978) "Long-term changes in the form of the city centre: the case of redevelopment", *Geogr. Annlr.* Ser. B. **60**, 79–96; Whitehand, J. W. R. (1979) "The study of variations in the building fabric of town centres: procedural problems and preliminary findings in southern Scotland", *Trans. Inst. Br. Geogr.* N.S. **4**, 559–75; Luffrum, J. M. (1980) "Variations in the building fabric of small towns", *Trans. Inst. Br. Geogr.* N.S. 5, 170–3.

89. Openshaw (1974b) op. cit. (note 85).

90. Ibid. p. 445.

91. Carter (1972) op. cit. p. 253 (note 2).

92. Corey, op. cit. (note 82).

93. Forster, C. A. (1972) "Court housing in Kingston upon Hull: an example of cyclic processes in the morphological development of nineteenth century bye-law housing", *Univ. of Hull Occ. Pap. Geogr.* **19**.

94. Whitehand (1977) op. cit. (note 38).

95. Forster, op. cit. p. 49 (note 93).

96. Johnston, R. J. (1968) "An outline of the development of Melbourne's street pattern", *Aust. Geogr.* **10**, 453–65.

97. Openshaw (1974b) op. cit. pp. 108–263 (note 85).

98. Millward, H. A. (1975) "The convergence of urban plan features: a comparative analysis of trends in Canada and England", unpubl. Ph.D. diss., Univ. of Western Ontario, pp. 36–41.

99. Ibid. p. 172.

100. Carter, H. (1976) "The geographical approach", in Barley (1976) op. cit. p. 17 (note 27).

101. Openshaw (1974b) op. cit. pp. 108–203 (note 85).

102. Barley (1976) op. cit. pp. 18–19 (note 27).

103. Openshaw (1974b) op. cit. p. 447 (note 85).

104. Barke (1976) op. cit. (note 40).

105. Whitehand (1972b) op. cit. (note 38); Whitehand (1974) op. cit. (note 38).

106. Carter, H. (1970) "A decision-making approach to town plan analysis: a case study of Llandudno", in Carter, H. and Davies, W. K. D. (eds) *Urban essays: studies in the geography of Wales* (London) p. 66.

107. Ibid. pp. 66–78.

108. Aspinall, P. J. and Whitehand, J. W. R. (1980) "Building plans: a major source for urban studies", *Area* **12**, 199–203; Aspinall, P. J. (1982) "The makers of the townscape: an evaluation of sources for historical research", *Dep. Geogr. Univ. of Birmingham Occ. Publs.* 15.

109. The *Social Science Citation Index* does not, of course, afford a comprehensive list of citations, being largely restricted to those appearing in major national and international journals.

110. Lowenthal, D. (1979) "Environmental perception: preserving the past", *Prog. Hum. Geogr.* **3**, 549–59. For a broad perspective on the recent history of attitudes to conservation in Britain see especially Harvey, J. (1972) *Conservation of buildings* (London) pp. 24–5, 36–40.

111. Linton, D. L. (1968) "The assessment of scenery as a natural resource", *Scott. geogr. Mag.* **84**, 219–38.

112. For a similar view see Conzen, M. P. (1978) "Analytical approaches to the urban landscape", *Univ. of Chicago Dep. Geogr. Res. Pap.* **186**, 137.

113. Allsop, B. (1974) *Towards a humane architecture* (London) pp. 54–5.

114. Banz, G. (1970) *Elements of urban form* (New York) p. 117.

115. Johns, op. cit. (note 2).

116. Vance, op. cit. (note 2). For a review of approaches to the urban landscape see Conzen, M. P. (1978) op. cit. (note 112).

117. For example, Hoskins, W. G. (1955) *The making of the English landscape* (London) esp. pp. 210–30.

118. For example, Beresford, M. (1957) *History on the ground* (London) esp. pp. 125–83; Beresford, M. (1967) *New towns of the middle ages: town plantation in England, Wales and Gascony* (London) pp. 142–78; Beresford, M. W. (1971) "The back-to-back house in Leeds, 1787–1937", in Chapman, S. D. (ed.) *The history of working-class housing* (Newton Abbot) pp. 93–132.

119. Dyos, H. J. (1968) "The speculative builders and developers of Victorian London", *Vict. Stud.* **11**, 641–90.

120. Openshaw (1974b) op. cit. (note 85).

121. Aspinall, P. J. (1978) "Building applications and the building industry in nineteenth century towns: the scope for statistical analysis", *Cent. Urb. Reg. Stud. Univ. of Birmingham Res. Mem.* **68**.

122. See Aspinall and Whitehand, op. cit. (note 108).

123. Openshaw (1974b) op. cit. p. 447 (note 85).

124. Conzen, M. R. G. (1958) "The growth and character of Whitby", in Daysh, G. H. J. (ed.) *A survey of Whitby and the surrounding area* (Eton) pp. 49–89. In this study comparatively little space is devoted to the town plan.

125. Conzen, M. P. (1978) op. cit. p. 135 (note 112).

126. Lewis, P. (1975) "To revive urban downtowns show respect for the spirit of the place", *Smithsonian* **6**, 32–41.

AUTHOR INDEX

References to footnotes are in italic

SUBJECT INDEX

References to footnotes are in italic